Gamesman Bridge

Play Better with Kantar

EDWIN B. KANTAR
AND JACKSON STANLEY

With a foreword by JIM JACOBY

Melvin Powers
Wilshire Book Company

12015 Sherman Road, No. Hollywood, CA 91605

 ISBN 0-87980-391-6
Library of Congress Catalog Card Number: 72-87099

Manufactured in the United States of America

CONTENTS

"Eddie Kantar is the world's best gamesman."
—WALTER BINGHAM, *Sports Illustrated*

"Anybody who plays as erratically as Stanley should never win, but Jack often does. I guess he's become a pretty good gamesman himself."
—EDWIN B. KANTAR

FOREWORD

There are two ways to do everything in this world, as anyone who has ever taken a finesse can testify—the right way and the wrong way. The same goes for teaching bridge. This highly original book shows what can happen to a bridge player who has been taught wrong. That happened to Jack Stanley, and he appealed to Eddie Kantar for help. The results of their sessions have been set down in dialogue form to provide a bridge book as entertaining as it is instructive.

Edwin B. Kantar has won two World Championships and has represented North America as both player and coach in International competition. He also holds over a dozen major National titles. He is a columnist and writer for leading bridge magazines and is recognized as one of the best and most entertaining of bridge teachers.

Jackson Stanley now deceased was a novelist and TV writer who began to play bridge the year Edwin Kantar was born. As he put it, he had been making mistakes all Mr. Kantar's life. He was taught to play by his father—an amusing tyrant at the table—and the bad habits he acquired will be instantly recognized by millions of bridge players.

The collaboration proves to be a Palooka's Odyssey, describing in detail Stanley's progress under Kantar's lash. It's a case history of a learning process, and the reader will be encouraged to see that problems which have puzzled him also puzzle others.

Kantar teaches Stanley what to lead and why and how to avoid taking unnecessary finesses. He teaches him to count, to draw inferences from his opponents bids and plays, and to improve communications with his partner.

At last Stanley makes modest progress. He learns to listen to the bidding and to count side suits as well as trumps. He brings off an end-play. On purpose. Then comes the climax. He plays with Kantar in a championship tournament and achieves the dream of every duplicate player, to sit with one of the greats for a full fifty-two boards of play! My partner, the expert!

Anyone who hasn't improved his bridge play after reading this book isn't really trying.

For my part, I was most entertained by Jack Stanley's description of the way his father taught him the game. Fortunately, my father didn't take the same approach. The difference, as Stanley graciously points out in the text, might not have been in the fathers, but in the sons. That's a nice compliment, but anyone who can't learn to play bridge from Oswald Jacoby isn't really trying.

JIM JACOBY

ONE

Philosophy of the gaffe

STANLEY: Contract bridge was a Sunday event in my father's house for many years until World War II absorbed most of the players. We always had two tables going, sometimes three. We were young, combative, and vocal. The game itself was young, its major prophets yet to come. Ely Culbertson was the reigning guru, and his Blue Book on Bidding and Red Book on Play were testaments whose word my father never questioned.

I have no idea how many hands of bridge I've played since then, nor how many hours I've spent hashing them over, but when this hand was dealt it became etched into the minds of the survivors, and a lifetime conversation piece:

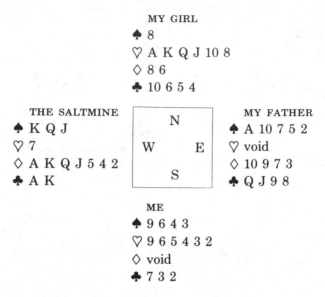

MY GIRL
♠ 8
♡ A K Q J 10 8
◊ 8 6
♣ 10 6 5 4

THE SALTMINE
♠ K Q J
♡ 7
◊ A K Q J 5 4 2
♣ A K

MY FATHER
♠ A 10 7 5 2
♡ void
◊ 10 9 7 3
♣ Q J 9 8

ME
♠ 9 6 4 3
♡ 9 6 5 4 3 2
◊ void
♣ 7 3 2

I held the Southern Yarborough, and Mildred, my fiancée, was my partner. Sitting West was a lean schoolmate of mine, a compulsive gambler who nowadays would be called a born loser. Robbie was cheerful and impulsive, ever confident that his fearful streak of bad luck would someday end. Recalling Dostoevski and the dreary Siberian wastes, we had dubbed him the Saltmine.

Robbie was playing with my father. It was not a salutary partnership. My father was splenetic and explosive at the bridge table. He accepted his partners as evidence of the wrath of God, like Job's boils. He was a seething volcano, as frightening before as during his eruptions.

After I passed, Robbie with his five honor tricks made the customary Culbertson forcing call of two diamonds. Mildred was a forthright young woman afraid of nothing. She bid two hearts.

My father now had a problem. He wanted to bid three hearts to show his void but was afraid Robbie would misinterpret this bidding refinement. He had sufficient trump support for a raise, but the possibility of playing the hand himself was not entirely out of the question since he had the master suit. Two spades showed one and one-half honor tricks so he bid it.

In the South seat I hesitated while Robbie waited impatiently for me to bid. I thought briefly of making an advance sacrifice but decided that these opponents were quite capable of fouling up, so I passed.

Robbie bid a Culbertson four notrump, showing either three aces or two aces and the king of a previously bid suit, and my father broke into a relieved smile. According to the system, a response of five notrump showed two aces. Now he felt he could show his void, the equivalent of the ace of hearts, by bidding five notrump!

I wanted to sacrifice again but thought I might have another crack at it. I passed, and Robbie didn't wait for the last sibilant to die before he said seven notrump. He was that sort of chap, always reaching for the stars. With his partner holding both aces, it was unthinkable to Robbie that he should bid his grand slam in anything so minor-league as diamonds!

Mildred sighed. The Saltmine never did anything right. She felt sorry for him. But not sorry enough to refrain from doubling. When the bidding came round to Robbie he redoubled.

My poor father. It had all become agonizingly clear. That oaf of a Robbie had taken the convention literally! My father's face became flushed and he popped perspiration. The penalty could be enormous, 400 for the first and 600 for each subsequent trick.

"I'm afraid there's been a breakdown in communication," he said, sadly, resorting at this moment of disaster to typical British understatement.

KANTAR: What he stated was the source of most disasters

in bridge. Since bridge is a partnership game, communication is all-important. The language is severely limited. You have eight nouns (notrump, spade, heart, diamond, club, double, redouble, and pass) and seven adjectives (one, two, three, four, five, six, and seven) which combine to form a total of only thirty-eight phrases with which to describe the 635,013,559,600 possible hands in bridge. You might bid your hands perfectly, but unless your partner understands what your bids mean, you might as well be talking to him in Urdu.

As a basic principle, I do suggest that you keep all your bidding simple. to cut down on the ambiguities, you and your partner might encounter. If you want potatoes, don't ask for *pommes de terre* unless you know your partner speaks French.

STANLEY: That's good advice, but I didn't introduce this hand to exploit the mistakes of my dear old dad. His wasn't the key mistake on the hand. The ultimate, classic gaffe was mine.

You see, before Mildred could run off her six good heart tricks to set the redoubled grand slam 3400 points, I led a heart out of turn!

My wife uttered an anguished scream, and Robbie, assured that his luck had changed at last, barred the heart lead. He spread the hand for a grand slam redoubled score of 3130, representing a swing I will never live down. 6530!

You'll notice I referred to Mildred as my wife. Yes, she married me. Where else could a girl find a husband who'd let her lead out of turn all her life without daring a word of criticism?

KANTAR: Nowhere! You must be an ideal partner.

STANLEY: Alas, I'm not! I still make mistakes, and then ruin the next three hands brooding about them. What I'd like from you is some kind of a system to improve my game.

KANTAR: No system in the world will make a good bridge player out of a bad one. All I can show you is what to look for in a hand, and suggest what do do with it when you find it. I can point out the advantages of *counting*, not just the trump suit, but every suit. I can show you all the newest ways of communicating with partner, and I think I could teach you how to draw inferences from opponents' bids, as well as to place missing cards. Most important of all, I would try to make you understand how important it is to *think*. You'd be surprised how easy it is to push thirteen cards onto the table without thinking at all.

STANLEY: I'm not a bit surprised. I do it all the time.

KANTAR: You floor me.

STANLEY: That's the whole problem. I was taught wrong from the start. I not only play a hand wrong, I think about it wrong. You have no idea what junk I have in my head when I pick up those thirteen cards.

KANTAR: I'd rather not hear about it.

STANLEY: Be brave. I'll tell you about it in the next chapter.

TWO

The basics in brief

STANLEY: Hollywood in the thirties was considered something of a Babylon, a city of sin, but according to my father most of the greatest sins of the time were committed at the bridge table.

Contract bridge caught on in the movie colony much like Mah-Jongg, miniature golf, and playing games with stock girls.

Among those who took up the game were a pair of my father's actor friends, Hob, a screen tough-guy, then in high favor for gangster roles, and Alfredo, an Italian character actor who portrayed Roman dukes, waiters, and organ grinders with equal Latin intensity. They challenged my father to a set game, and though he warned them that they would be no match for him, they had the hubris of born actors and showed up in full confidence of victory.

I was flattered when my father invited me to play as his partner, assuming my game had improved to meet his absurdly high standards. But no. He was less interested in my ability than my consanguinity.

"They're begging for it," he said. "It would be conspicuous waste not to keep all the money in the family."

Before they arrived, my father stressed the importance of keeping out of trouble while playing a set game.

"Don't take chances. Push them beyond their depth, but don't take sacrifices. If the rubber belongs to them, let them have it. We'll get it all back on the next deal." This was strange advice coming from a man I had seen take 800-point sets to keep his opponents from scoring 500-point rubbers, but in this case there was something far more important than prestige at stake. Money.

"Play slowly and don't make any wild bids," he cautioned.

"Fair enough," I said. "I'll do my best. But please don't yell at me. You make me so nervous criticizing my play that I make mistakes three hands later."

"Don't worry. I'll treat you like a Ming vase."

Hob and Alfredo arrived, their hands itching for the cards. Though my father was equally eager to play, he demonstrated a fine show of British diffidence. Knowing his enthusiasm for the game, and his high expectation of winning, I thought his insouciance showed a talent for acting his guests might well have envied.

Many months before, after suffering from the inadequacies of less-gifted partners, my father had issued a set of basic rules he expected to be followed by anyone who played with him. He scrawled his commandments on a shirtboard which loomed over our mantelpiece on Sundays till in the end, much handled and smudged, it became as gray and round-cornered as the Tablet itself. Being more messianic even than Moses, he came up with eleven commandments instead of ten.

Despite the elementary nature of my father's injunctions, I was astonished to see that Hob and Alfredo violated them all! Not only that—I've been watching other players make the same mistakes for years.

1. Thou shalt not lead singleton kings. Hob did it twice. The first time I'd otherwise have had to take a losing finesse. Next time he did it, his partner had the ace. Alfredo naturally signaled high, and Hob's frantic attempts to get his partner in the lead so he could ruff gave me the tempo I needed to bring in an unmakable game.

2. Thou shalt not underlead aces against suit contracts. This commandment, which may be broken when your opponents' stronger hand is to your left, was often violated by Alfredo who thought underleading aces was quite clever.

3. Thou shalt not finesse thy partner's lead. Hob and Alfredo did it repeatedly, conducting their defensive strategy on the same individualistic foundations that made our country great. But what makes for good countries makes for lousy bridge. They were what my father called Thirteen-Card Defenders, forgetting that as a team they had twenty-six cards on their side. They frequently misplayed this combination at notrump contracts:

DUMMY: ◊ 8 7 2

HOB LEADS: ◊ 3   ALFREDO: ◊ K J 6

Instead of playing the king, Alfredo thought he might steal something by coming up with the jack. On the occasions when declarer held the ace, no harm was done, nor was there anything gained. But when declarer held ◊ Q 5 4, the play of the jack lost a needless trick.

Since they were so reluctant to play their big cards when it was correct, I would have expected them to cope well with the situation when it was like this:

DUMMY: ♠ J 7 2

ALFREDO LEADS: ♠ 3   HOB: ♠ K 10 6

If the dummy plays small, Hob's correct play of course is the ten, keeping his king master over the jack. But Hob didn't see it that way. "I never finesse my partner's lead," he'd say, blasting with his king. This meant an extra trick for declarer holding something like ♠ A 9 5.

4. *Thou shalt lead the top of equals but take tricks with the lowest of equals.*

DUMMY: ♡ 8 7 6

HOB LEADS: ♡ 10 ALFREDO PLAYS: ♡ K

ME: ♡ A 5 4

At first I didn't believe they could hold any possible combination of cards where the lead and Alfredo's play made any sense. Singleton ten? Then Alfredo with ♡ K Q J 9 3 2 would have overtaken with the jack. Singleton king? Then Hob with ♡ Q J 10 9 3 2 would have led the queen. Finally I reasoned that Hob was leading the top of an interior sequence ♡ Q 10 9 and that Alfredo had the ♡ K J.

It wasn't like that at all. Our actors had fractured this commandment both ways at once. Hob had ♡ J 10 9 3 (and should have led top of a sequence, the jack) while Alfredo had the ♡ K Q 2 (and should have unblocked his queen.)

I wanted to tell them the correct way of playing these combinations, but my father silenced me with a warning scowl. He had acquired a wise reluctance to dispense free advice to the enemy.

5. *Thou shalt not make the false finesse.* Having been schooled against it early in life, I thought it was never done. But no. Here was Hob in action.

DUMMY: ♣ A 3 2

HOB: ♣ Q 5 4

Instead of leading from dummy toward his queen, hoping to find the king on his right, Hob found a side-suit entry into his hand and actually led the queen toward the ace! I'd have covered with the king if I'd had it, of course, but was forced to play small. When my father won the trick with his king, Hob groaned.

"You guys are murderin' me; I haven't made a finesse all night."

"You didn't make one that time, either," said my father, his fine British irony unrecognized.

6. *Thou shalt not play second hand high.* Alfredo was particularly extravagant with his intermediate cards in second position, this being a typical example.

DUMMY: ♠ K 7 5 2

ALFREDO: ♠ Q 10 4   HOB: ♠ A 8 3

ME: ♠ J 9 6

I led the six, Alfredo put in the ten with his inevitable battle-cry, "Not through the iron duke!" followed by the king and ace. Hob returned the eight and I gave up only two tricks whereas I should have lost the top three against this combination if Alfredo could have eschewed his ducal prerogative.

This particular blind spot of Alfredo's inspired my father to make an observation after the game which history has proven to be somewhat less than prophetic:

"Italians don't have the temperament for contract bridge."

7. *Thou shalt not overtake partner's good tricks.* There is much to be said, of course, for the violation of any Messiah's Seventh Commandment, but my father permitted exceptions only from those who knew what they were doing. When Hob and Alfredo overtook or trumped partner's good tricks—they didn't!

8. *Thou shalt not necessarily cover an honor with an honor.* Hob and Alfredo misunderstood this commandment completely, holding with religious fervor to the conviction that should an honor appear on the table, they had to smash it with one higher. It's hardly necessary for me to describe the numerous hands where they eased our weary way through a torturous undergrowth of missing high cards. On the few occasions when they refused to cover, consistency being the least of their faults in play, their hesitation was so painful, sincere, and time-consuming that the missing honor might as well have been exposed face-up on the table.

9. *Thou shalt not become blocked in the wrong hand.* My father's instructions in this department had been bellowed at me from earliest childhood. But Hob hadn't been there to learn:

DUMMY: ♡ Q J 9 8

HOB: ♡ A K 4

The contract was three notrump, and I had led the three of hearts from ♡ 10 7 6 3 2. Hob put in the eight from the table, and when it held, carelessly played the four from his hand. (The only time he ever overtook a good trick was when his partner played it!) He then cashed tricks in all his side suits until it became apparent he had exhausted his entries to his fourth heart in dummy.

10. *Thou shalt use thy small trumps in dummy to trump losers from thy hand.* This was elementary, but Hob and Alfredo lost countless tricks by prematurely drawing trumps. The most blatant example of this weakness occurred near the end of the evening. (As for the bidding, well, it was fairly shaggy, too!)

North-South vulnerable
South dealer

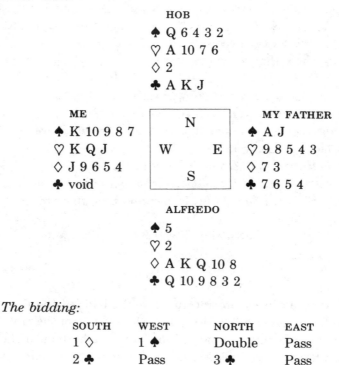

HOB
♠ Q 6 4 3 2
♡ A 10 7 6
◊ 2
♣ A K J

ME
♠ K 10 9 8 7
♡ K Q J
◊ J 9 6 5 4
♣ void

MY FATHER
♠ A J
♡ 9 8 5 4 3
◊ 7 3
♣ 7 6 5 4

ALFREDO
♠ 5
♡ 2
◊ A K Q 10 8
♣ Q 10 9 8 3 2

The bidding:

SOUTH	WEST	NORTH	EAST
1 ◊	1 ♠	Double	Pass
2 ♣	Pass	3 ♣	Pass
5 ♣	All pass		

I led the king of hearts. Alfredo took the ace on the table, trumped a heart in his hand, led a trump, and groaned when he discovered I was void. He won with the jack of clubs on the table (breaking the Ninth Commandment) pulled two more trumps with the ace-king, and came to hand by trumping another heart. He pulled the last trump and then seemed surprised when he had to lose two diamond tricks, in addition to his singleton spade.

"I had to bid it," said Alfredo, mournfully. "They probably make one spade doubled."

GAMESMAN BRIDGE

Since it was unlikely at this late hour that they could learn enough to hurt us, my father deigned to teach them something. "You could have made seven if you had used your small trumps in dummy to take care of your losing diamonds."

"But I didn't have any small trumps in dummy," said Alfredo, remembering how grateful he had been to see the ace-king-jack.

My father shrugged. "Small is relative. But then—you would have made only six unless you remembered to unblock by trumping with your two *largest* small trumps in dummy."

Hob and Alfredo were anxious to get on to the next hand, but I saw what my father was talking about. My lead of the king of hearts would have enabled Alfredo to ruff out my queen and jack with his ace and king of trumps, discarding his losing spade on the established ten of hearts in dummy. Holding a trump, I could have ruffed, but since I was void, seven was cold if he had preserved the jack of clubs as a re-entry to his hand.

11. Thou shalt win thy tricks in proper season. My father had an entrenched preference for notrump contracts, not alone because they required fewer tricks for game, but because he believed them more difficult for the defence.

"Inexperienced players take their winners too soon," he said, "enabling you to establish your small cards without a struggle." Then he laughed, adding, "Funny part of it is, when they play against suit contracts, they don't take their tricks soon enough. They marry their aces, hoping they'll reproduce."

Neither vulnerable
North dealer

ME
♠ A K 10 2
♡ Q 10 9
◇ 3 2
♣ A K Q J

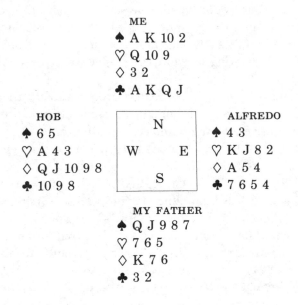

HOB
♠ 6 5
♡ A 4 3
◇ Q J 10 9 8
♣ 10 9 8

ALFREDO
♠ 4 3
♡ K J 8 2
◇ A 5 4
♣ 7 6 5 4

MY FATHER
♠ Q J 9 8 7
♡ 7 6 5
◇ K 7 6
♣ 3 2

The bidding:

NORTH	SOUTH
1 ♣	1 ♠
4 ♠	All pass

"Hob led the queen of diamonds," my father recounted, "and Alfredo should have been able to see I had ten tricks on top—at least four spades, four clubs, the king of diamonds, and a diamond ruff in dummy. His only hope was to go up with the ace of diamonds and switch to a heart. But no. He saved that ace for his scrapbook."

Despite the extraordinary deficiencies of our adversaries, we came toward the end of the evening not ahead of them—but behind! The reason was not difficult to find. Though in the long run we should have beaten Alfredo and Hob easily, we had access to them for no more than a short run. And the law of averages had been supplanted by the law of compensation. To balance their inexperience, Alfredo and Hob drew all the cards!

My father became disconsolate, but not alone because of our bad luck. Since he equated a well-played hand of bridge with a work of art, he suffered miseries at the thought of the destruction our Thespians were inflicting on their blockbuster hands. Then, during the final rubber, his spirits picked up.

We set them twice in the last rubber, became vulnerable, and then along came this hand.

North-South vulnerable
South dealer

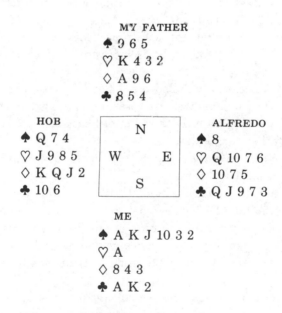

MY FATHER
♠ 9 6 5
♡ K 4 3 2
◇ A 9 6
♣ 8 5 4

HOB
♠ Q 7 4
♡ J 9 8 5
◇ K Q J 2
♣ 10 6

ALFREDO
♠ 8
♡ Q 10 7 6
◇ 10 7 5
♣ Q J 9 7 3

ME
♠ A K J 10 3 2
♡ A
◇ 8 4 3
♣ A K 2

The bidding:

SOUTH	NORTH
1 ♠	1 NT
4 ♠	All pass

Hob led the king of diamonds, and as my father put down the dummy he said, "This has been one hell of an evening. Thank God it's over." He then mentally added the score, and from his grin of satisfaction I could see that we had tottered through the valley of the shadow and were still among the land of the living.

As was my custom in those days I glanced briefly at the dummy and counted ten winners even if I should fail to pick up the queen of spades. I took the ace of diamonds on the board and then quickly played the ace and king of trumps in the expectation of dropping the queen. My father, you see, in order to spare me the agony of thinking had provided me with a cabalistic phrase to cover the situation when holding the ace-king of a suit, missing the queen. With eight cards I was to finesse, with nine, play for the drop. "Eight ever, nine never" was the way this banal little rhyme went, and I put my faith in it completely.

On this occasion it failed me. I not only lost the queen of trumps and two diamonds, but I was unable to get to the board to sack my losing club on the king of hearts.

My father turned purple.

"Why didn't you give up a trick to the queen of spades?"

"You said if I had nine——"

"Ye gods, I've raised a bloody parrot! Couldn't you see the hand was foolproof whether you picked up the queen or not, just as long as you had the nine of spades as an entry to the board? Once the queen of spades was gone and you had un-blocked your ace of hearts, the nine of trumps was as high as your ace!"

So what happened? Instead of escaping the grim evening with a small loss, our bad cards returned to us and the actors ran off a game and a vulnerable slam. We had counted our pigeons before they were hatched.

KANTAR: Perhaps one of the things that did you in was trying to play bridge with the aid of nursery rhymes. Your father's eleven commandments covered the basics for beginners but that stuff about "eight ever, nine never" makes me ill.

STANLEY: A man has to have some kind of slogan to live by. You know, like "Be Prepared" and "Fight Smog."

KANTAR: I'll buy that.

STANLEY: Since you feel that way about helpful hints, perhaps you'll have something to say about another slogan my father laid on me: "Never take the first finesse."

KANTAR: I'm not sure I know what that means—but I bet it's madness!

THREE

The first finesse

STANLEY: I'm only human. Rather than blame my bad bridge on myself, I blame it on my teacher. The phrase "generation gap" hadn't been invented then, but you don't have to know the name of a disease to suffer from it.

My father, patiently trying to instill in me the rudiments of the game, couldn't understand how such an idiot could have been born into his brilliant family. I brooded at the social injustice of permitting an old man—he was all of forty-three—to live beyond his usefulness. Our harsh appraisal of each other was increased, not lessened, by our normal ties of affection. You always hurt the one you love, notably at the bridge table.

Whenever we were partners the auction became a sort of miniature war in which one of the allies had to be slain before the stronger of the two could take on the enemy.

North-South vulnerable
East dealer

MY FATHER
♠ A 4
♡ Q 9 3 2
◇ A Q J
♣ K 7 6 3

ME
♠ 10 9
♡ K J 10 8 7
◇ 6 5 4
♣ A Q 8

The bidding:

SOUTH (ME)	NORTH (MY FATHER)
1 ♡ *	3 NT **
4 ♡ ***	All pass ****

* A typical Culbertson opening, two and a half honor tricks.

** We have a game here, son. Just sit back and I'll take care of everything.

*** He won't be able to stand the pointy suits, and I ought to have the lead come up to my ace-queen of clubs. His notrump doesn't deny hearts, it merely affirms his bull-headedness. Fact is, I rather expect he has the ace and queen both.

**** I give up! To think, he was all twisted up in his umbilical cord and I set him free!

The opening lead was the trey of diamonds.

As any contract bridge player knows, it is the responsibility

THE FIRST FINESSE   19 of the loser who has been elected dummy to put his cards face up on the table, the trumps first and the other suits haphazardly as they come to hand.

My father tabled the following:

♠ A 4 ♡ Q 9 3 ◇ A Q J [2] ♣ K 7 6 3

You will note that this fails to correspond to the hand I showed above. My father was pretending the deuce of hearts had accidentally become mixed up with his diamonds, thus giving him an excuse for not responding in my suit.

So much for the inferential histrionics. From then on, all the dramatics were verbal and physical.

As soon as the hand went down and without inspecting it carefully I decided that we had probably underbid. The only guaranteed loser I had was the ace of trumps. With an adolescent glare at my father for having bulled us out of an easy small slam I played the jack of diamonds from the dummy.

East produced the king and returned the four before bothering to gather in his trick. My father made gasping sounds and clutched the bottom half of his jaw as if it might fall off into his lap. Although I must admit my father was a good card player, above average on defense and superior as declarer, as dummy he was lousy.

I won the second trick on the table with the queen of diamonds, now being irritated at my father for being smart enough to stop short of an unmakable slam. I led a trump to knock out the ace, prepared to spread the hand for a claim of five as soon as it dropped. West won, and stolidly continued diamonds, to the ace in the dummy.

East had a surprise. He trumped.

Now, with three tricks already in the coffers of the opposition I felt a cold wave of anxiety. This slam hand of mine wasn't even a certain game! I still had a spade to lose unless I could plant it on the thirteenth club.

While all this was going on, my father's actions suggested that he had missed his calling in life. He was miscast as a journalist; he should have been a tragedian. When my ace of diamonds was trumped, he raised his eyes to heaven and with his ten fingers pointing upward begged his Maker for succor, or at least instant deliverance from this world of infinite fallibility. Finally, as the speed of my play slowed to a pace that any dummy recognizes as connoting disaster, my father sank into his chair with his face buried in his hands like somebody had just run over his dog.

Needless to say, or I wouldn't be mentioning it here, the clubs split normally, which is to say, 4-2, and I went down one.

I knew my father's torpor couldn't last. As I wrote down the score, he bounded out of his seat, his face flaming and his eyes a pair of beady, blue bombs. "You muttonhead! If I've told you once, I've told you a million times! Never take the first finesse!"

So that's how I learned to play bridge. At the wrong end of a bull-horn.

The scene changed. It was thirty years later. I was playing in an open pairs duplicate tournament sponsored by Omar Sharif and his Flying Circus. I was playing South and my left-hand opponent was Jim Jacoby, who had also learned to play bridge at his father's knee, but with altogether different results. Perhaps it was because Oswald had an altogether different son!

My partner was Connie Kirkendall. Although she is a bridge teacher, we were playing as friends. She made no attempt to teach me anything, and I promised not to learn anything.

Both vulnerable
North dealer

♠ J 8 4
♡ A Q 7
◇ A 4 3
♣ K Q 8 2

♠ A K 10 5 3 2
♡ 8 6
◇ K 9
♣ A 5 4

The bidding:

NORTH	SOUTH (ME)
1 NT	3 ♠
3 NT	4 NT
5 ♡	6 ♠
All pass	

Jacoby led the heart four and once again I was confronted with an immediate problem: to finesse or not to finesse.

I suppose it's natural to blame my father for everything. I could hear his voice ringing down the corridors of time and I went up with the ace.

The clubs didn't break (again!) and Jacoby had three trumps to the queen, as well as the king of hearts.

Down one!

So how can you account for the fact that I haven't improved in thirty years?

KANTAR: Because in all that time you never once thought you had to *think*.

Take your first hand.

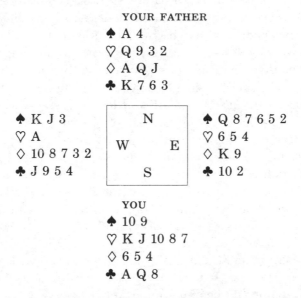

YOUR FATHER
♠ A 4
♡ Q 9 3 2
♢ A Q J
♣ K 7 6 3

♠ K J 3
♡ A
♢ 10 8 7 3 2
♣ J 9 5 4

N
W   E
S

♠ Q 8 7 6 5 2
♡ 6 5 4
♢ K 9
♣ 10 2

YOU
♠ 10 9
♡ K J 10 8 7
♢ 6 5 4
♣ A Q 8

When the three of diamonds was led, you gave some thought to the hand, i.e., that you had missed a slam, but that's what I mean when I say that more often than not you think of the wrong things. Then, quickly, you took that first finesse.

Right now you must agree to renounce the bad habits you have cultivated in thirty years of impetuous play. When you are declarer and dummy goes down, the first order of business is to *think*. If your loose hand begins to creep toward dummy, sit on it. Tie it to the chair, even stick it in your mouth and bite off all your nails, but don't touch the dummy till you have *finished* thinking.

There's a lot to think about.

1. What is the meaning of the lead?
2. How many losers do I have?

THE FIRST FINESSE

23

3. Does the enemy bidding (or lack of it!) help you count distribution and place high cards in the enemy hands?

In this hand there was no adverse bidding, so you had no clues to your opponents' distribution. You should then have counted your losers. You figured to lose the ace of trumps, maybe one spade, and maybe the king of diamonds. Since you can afford three losers to make your contract you ought to be home, but that's no excuse for you to stop thinking. There are pitfalls in the safest of hands, as you well know.

Analyze the lead. A small-card lead suggests a lead from length, and is usually fourth best of the suit. Since he also might have held the deuce, you could then assume that West led from four or five diamonds, and East, therefore, held the remaining three or two. As for the missing high cards in the suit—all you had to worry about was the king. If the opening leader had it, you had no problem, as you could always pick it up by finessing. But if East held it, you were bound to lose it.

In many hands, it doesn't matter whether you lose your tricks early or late, but whenever you lack the ace or king of trumps, timing can be quite important.

As the cards lay, your father was quite correct: it was fatal to take the first finesse. But if West had led from the K 8 7 3 2, it could have been fatal *not* to take the finesse, for with the ace of trumps out, a diamond ruff was still possible.

The point about this hand is that you should be alive to its dangers before you make any impetuous play. You might have guessed wrong after giving it careful thought, but your downfall would have come from the lie of the cards, not because of some cabalistic nonsense about not taking the first finesse! By filling your head with slogans, your father clogged it for thinking purposes. He failed to differentiate between hands depending on judgment and those where it was technically wrong to finesse.

Explore this one, for example. The contract is six hearts, and you're confronted with the opening lead of the four of spades.

♠ A Q 2
♡ A J 7 6
◇ 9 8
♣ K 10 5 4

♠ 6 5
♡ K Q 10 3 2
◇ A K Q
♣ A J 4

Think about this hand carefully. What do you see? A possible spade loser, and a possible club loser. If you take the spade finesse and lose it, you'll still have to guess who has the queen of clubs.

Is there a better way?

Yes. This time your father's advice happens to be right. Refuse the finesse. Take the ace of spades. Draw trumps. (Even if they are split 3-1, you'll still have one in dummy.) Play your diamonds, throwing a spade from dummy. Then play the queen of spades, not caring who wins.

Now sit back and wait for either a club return or a ruff, and a sluff. With either return the contract is assured.

Now then, let's go back to your hand in the open pairs tournament and see if we can apply reason, not slogans, to solving the problem.

♠ J 8 4
♡ A Q 7
◇ A 4 3
♣ K Q 8 2

JACOBY
♠ Q 7 6
♡ K 10 5 4
◇ Q 10 7 6
♣ 9 7

♠ 9
♡ J 9 3 2
◇ J 8 5 2
♣ J 10 6 3

YOU
♠ A K 10 5 3 2
♡ 8 6
◇ K 9
♣ A 5 4

Count the hand. You have nine trumps but are missing the queen—you could lose a trick there. This pesky king of hearts—you could find it offside, too. No diamond losers, no club losers.

Once again it appears you have two finesses to take, and if you guess right on either one, you make your contract.

Ask yourself once again: Is there a better way?

In this case there's a way to avoid one finesse, but it's not better. You have seven clubs to the ace, king, queen. If the opposing clubs split 3-3 you'd be able to discard your losing heart on your thirteenth club.

But you have only a 36 percent chance of an even-up club split when there are six out against you, whereas the finesse is a straight fifty-fifty chance.

STANLEY: OK, OK. I understand you completely. This is one time I should have taken the first finesse. The percentages were all in its favor. But you're forgetting the human element. People hate to lead away from kings!

KANTAR: No, I haven't forgotten. When I tell some of the ladies I teach in my afternoon class to lead from a king, I have to reach over and pull the lead out of their hands. Then, half the time, they reach up and pull it right back! So it's true. With certain left-hand opponents you could be absolutely certain the king was on your right.

But not with Jim Jacoby on opening lead. You must not only analyze the lead, you must analyze the leader. Jacoby is one of the world's leading players, and I don't mean that as a pun.

Go back and listen to the bidding. Your partner opened one notrump. You carried on to slam.

Consider Jacoby's plight. He had seven high-card points. He knew his partner's hand was virtually empty, and his own good cards were finessable under that strong dummy. So Jim led a heart. He put you to the guess early. You went for it; you make your expected mistake.

I'm sure you realize that with any other lead, your slam was guaranteed. You couldn't miss. You'd stumble into it by accident. With either a club or a diamond lead, you'd lead trumps and discover the trump loser. Then you'd try your 36 percent club play, and when that failed you'd be *forced* to try the heart finesse, which Jim guessed from the beginning was a winner for you and a loser for him!

STANLEY: You make it all sound so easy. And so obvious. But for me to do that—I'm afraid you're expecting miracles. When I'm declarer I don't break down my thinking like that. I do it all by instinct. I don't count the tricks one by one. If I see a lot of high cards and a long suit or two I *feel* I have ten or eleven tricks in there and away I go!

KANTAR: You're like someone who is sick saying to his doctor: "Don't mess around with pills, doc—I'm a dead man!" I don't think you play as instinctively as you say—and if you do, that's why you lose!

For instance, how would your instinct tell you to play this hand? It came up in a sectional tournament and was bid in almost as many ways as there were players.

Match points
Both vulnerable
South dealer

♠ 4 3
♡ A Q 10 2
◊ A Q 2
♣ J 9 4 3

♠ K Q 2
♡ K J
◊ J 10 4 3
♣ A Q 10 2

GAMESMAN BRIDGE

The bidding:

SOUTH	WEST	NORTH	EAST
1 NT	2 ♠	3 ♠	Pass
3 NT	All pass		

Don't be confused by North's bid of three spades. It's Stayman, guaranteeing a game-going hand with at least four cards in the other major.

Three notrump is a logical contract, and with the opening lead of the jack of spades, how would you handle the play of the hand?

STANLEY: Well, now that I've had a lesson in thinking I'd stop and try to think what to think.

I'd analyze the lead. The jack is certainly the top of a sequence, with a strong probability that the ace lies upstairs. Then, a review of the bidding tells me more. The opening leader bid two spades vulnerable over my strong notrump. He undoubtedly has the spade ace, as well as the oustanding minor suit kings, for my partner and I have everything else.

I figure to take one spade, four top hearts, and three tricks each in the minors after I've knocked out the kings. Of course if I could win both finesses, I'd make thirteen, but since I assume West to have both kings, I'd rather not take the gamble. Why not go for one spade, four hearts, four diamonds, and the ace of clubs for an overtrick. I'll give him his king of clubs at the end. Right now, I'll take the diamond finesse.

KANTAR: Ugh! What's that your father called you? Button-brain? This hand is undefeatable with any lie of the cards, but as soon as you take the diamond finesse you go down two!

THE FIRST FINESSE   29

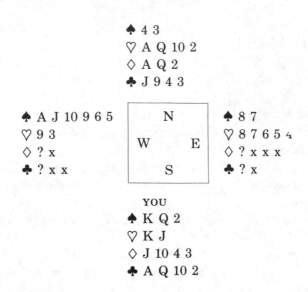

```
                    ♠ 4 3
                    ♡ A Q 10 2
                    ◊ A Q 2
                    ♣ J 9 4 3

♠ A J 10 9 6 5          N          ♠ 8 7
♡ 9 3                              ♡ 8 7 6 5 4
◊ ? x            W          E      ◊ ? x x x
♣ ? x x                 S          ♣ ? x

                   YOU
                    ♠ K Q 2
                    ♡ K J
                    ◊ J 10 4 3
                    ♣ A Q 10 2
```

You'll notice that I put question marks in the East and West
hands to designate the missing minor suit kings. When you take
the diamond finesse, I'll pop that king into East's hand in order
to teach you this lesson. I'm sure you can see what happens.
East wins with the king and leads back a spade, through your
stopper, and West runs off his strong suit, setting you two.

Now, just to be mean, what if I give you another losing
finesse by putting the king of *clubs* in West's hand. How would
losing the club finesse affect you?

STANLEY: My gosh, not at all! West will win and lead a
spade, but I still have a spade stopper.

KANTAR: Perhaps it's my fault you're able to blow a hand
like this. I taught you to think about pitfalls, and then admitted
there were many hands in which you could do nothing about
them. That's true—but there are others where, when you isolate
the danger, you can avoid it. You must realize that it is West
who has a long spade suit, but it is only dangerous if East gets
the lead. You should imagine a flashing red light over East's

head, and build your entire campaign around the tactic of keeping East out of the lead.

With this hand, it's quite easy, really. Facing two minor suit finesses, it should be obvious to choose the one leading you *away* from danger. When you lead the club, you don't care whether you win or lose the finesse—your contract is assured. If West clears the spades, you can take the other finesse later, once again not caring whether you win or lose, for East, with no more spades, is now about as dangerous as a kitten.

STANLEY: That's all so obvious! I should have been able to figure that out for myself.

KANTAR: Much of what I intend to tell you about bridge is obvious, but only when you've been taught to see it. For instance, *counting*. In playing this hand you seemed blissfully oblivious to the danger presented by West's long spade suit. You seemed to feel that he had high-card points in order to make a vulnerable overcall at the two-level, but you paid no attention to the more realistic assumption that he had a long suit and perhaps not as many high-card points as you thought.

STANLEY: You seem to forget that when I was taught to play bridge, the only thing we counted was honor tricks.

KANTAR: Unthinkable. Yet I happen to know you are right. As proof, look at this statement by Louis H. Watson in his otherwise impeccable classic, *The Play of the Hand at Bridge*. He wrote in 1934:

> Curiously, however, *teaching* would-be players to count is practically an impossibility. Since "counting" in Bridge is somewhat more than one, two, three, etc., being applied to each of the four suits and also to each of the four hands, it requires a logical mind, a great deal of patience (or what might be called dogged determination), and a certain amount of imagination. Without these qualities, a person can never become a great player anyway, so that it may also be said that without these qualities, a person cannot learn to *count*.

This is no longer true. Teaching methods have improved to the point that beginning players are taught to count opponents' distributions in the same lesson they're taught to count trumps. A well-instructed novice today *thinks* about a hand better than you do, because he's more concerned about distribution.

STANLEY: OK, I'm game. Teach me how to become an aging novice.

FOUR

Count, Count, COUNT!

KANTAR: I'd like to be able to tell you that you'll improve your ability to count a bridge hand by reading this chapter, but I'm afraid that simply wouldn't be true. I can give you a blueprint, and haul out some shining examples, but the only way you can learn to count is by doing it. Not occasionally, but on every single hand you play. The hardest part will be in remembering to do it, because you have stored up some of the worst bridge habits I've ever encountered. But once you've disciplined yourself to count automatically, you'll increase your enjoyment and play better.

East-West vulnerable
South dealer

♠ J 3 2
♡ 1 0 4 3
◇ K J 10
♣ 8 7 2

YOU
♠ 8 6
♡ A K Q 7 5
◇ A 4 2
♣ K Q J

The bidding:

SOUTH	WEST	NORTH	EAST
1 ♡	2 ♠	Pass	Pass
Double	Pass	3 ♡	Pass
4 ♡	All pass		

West's opening lead was the king of spades, followed by the queen. When he played the ace, East dropped the five of diamonds and you trumped. You drew trumps, noting that West held three. You then tackled clubs, West winning and returning a club. I hope you've been counting, because if you have, you can make this contract easy!

    STANLEY: West started with six spades and three trumps. He has now shown up with two clubs, totaling eleven, so his other two cards——

    KANTAR: Pardon the interruption. Counting the hand doesn't mean just sitting there letting things happen to you!

GAMESMAN BRIDGE

You're entitled to help yourself out. In fact, part of the technique is to lead safe suits for the *purpose* of getting the count. So will you please throw that last good club on the table! When you do, you'll see that West has followed with the ten of clubs.

STANLEY: I get it! With only one card unaccounted for in West's hand, he can't have more than one diamond!

KANTAR: Stop shouting! You sound as if you had just discovered the Pacific Ocean. Try to show a little restraint. On this hand, obviously, you lead to the king of diamonds and finesse on the way back.

Here are the East-West hands.

Notice that instinctively you started your count with the suit you knew about—spades. The principle is to count the hand holding the longest suit, because when you subtract from thirteen it's easier to handle a small remainder than a large one.

Try this hand.

Neither vulnerable
South dealer

♠ J 9 4 3
♡ Q 3
◇ A K 8
♣ A J 9 4

YOU
♠ K Q 10 8 7
♡ 9 5
◇ 6 3
♣ K 7 6 5

The bidding:

SOUTH	WEST	NORTH	EAST
Pass	4 ♡	Double	Pass
4 ♠	All pass		

West leads the king and ace of hearts (East echoing high-low) and then shifts to the jack of diamonds. You win in dummy and lead a small spade. East leaps in with the ace, you and West following, and then leads the queen of diamonds. You shudder at the thought of a ruff, but West discards a heart! Now then, quick as a wink, what is West's distribution?

STANLEY: Seven hearts, one diamond, one spade, and four clubs.

KANTAR: You've got it! It's unnecessary to show the East-West hands, but here they are.

♠ 2
♡ A K J 10 7 4 2
◇ J
♣ Q 10 3 2

N
W   E
S

♠ A 6 5
♡ 8 6
◇ Q 10 9 7 5 4 2
♣ 8

Any time you run into a freakish distribution, you'll find it relatively easy to get a count on the hand. Whenever an opponent shows out, it's unforgivable not to picture the original distribution of that suit. As soon as West showed out of diamonds you visualized seven diamonds in East's hand. When West failed to ruff a diamond you were able to judge the distribution of both hands with chilling accuracy. Your play is to draw trumps and play the king of clubs and a low club to the nine! Then return to your hand to take the marked club finesse against West's guarded queen. Practice counting whether the information is important to you or not.

You should automatically make a rough estimate of the enemy distribution, as well as your partner's, during the bidding. When the dummy goes down you should reassess your count and then clinch it whenever anyone shows out of a suit. Certain bids are shining beacons to give you a count on the enemy hands, the most notorious being the so-called "short club." Once it becomes apparent that the person who bid one club only has three, you may safely assume that the distribution will invariably be 4-3-3-3 or 4-4 in the majors with a doubleton diamond. Preemptive bids provide quick counts, since they are generally made on suits of six or more cards. When an opponent bids successively diamonds-clubs-clubs, you can figure at the most a total of three cards in the major suits, or after spades-hearts-

COUNT, COUNT, COUNT!

hearts, you should assume no more than three cards in the minors. The clues fly thick and fast during most auctions, but few players give the time and effort necessary to assimilate them.

Any time an opponent breaks a new suit, the card he leads will usually tell you what both he and his partner have in that suit. This is particularly true on opening lead where it pays to be honest. An experienced player avoids making plays that mislead partner!

Assume, for instance, that West leads an honor card. It will usually be the top of a sequence, and though you cannot tell immediately how *many* cards he has, you will automatically visualize the missing honors, not in dummy or your hand, as being with East.

Occasionally you'll be able to detect that such an honor card is a short-suit lead. If the opening leader comes out with a jack, which is normally from J 10 9, J 10 8, or sometimes J 10 x, and you have the ten in your hand or dummy, you *know* the lead is either a singleton or doubleton. The same applies if a queen is led and you can see the jack, or the jack turns up later in the opposite hand.

Leads of smaller cards call for a different type of detective work. Most leads of small cards are either fourth highest or low from three to an honor, except, of course, in suits that the opening leader's partner has bid.

What does fourth highest mean? It means that the opening leader has exactly three cards higher than the one he has led. So let's assume it was a deuce. You know immediately that the leader has exactly a four-card suit, with three cards higher than the one he has led.

But suppose he leads a three. You know that the leader has three cards higher than the three, but he can also have one lower! If he holds the deuce he has a five-card suit; but if you can see the deuce or the opening leader's partner plays it on the first trick, you know he must be leading from a four-card suit. This brings to mind two related points:

First, when a player leads high-low—for example, the three and then the deuce—he may have a three-deuce doubleton or he may be showing a five-card suit. Both partner and declarer should be able to read which it is through the bidding or inspection of the outstanding cards in hand and dummy.

Second, if the three is led and the declarer has the deuce in his own hand he knows something that his right-hand opponent does not. He knows that the opening leader started with a four-card suit, but the partner, not seeing the deuce, might think it was a five-card suit. Therefore, as declarer, any time you can conceal a card lower than the one led, you are making it more difficult for your RHO to count the hand.

Note how important this can be.

DUMMY: ♠ A K 7

WEST: ♠ J 9 8 3   EAST: ♠ 10 5 4

YOU: ♠ Q 6 2

You're in a heart contract, and West leads the three of spades. You have the deuce, so you assume West began with four spades and East three. East, however, can't see the deuce and doesn't know whether his partner started with four or five spades.

You win the spade in dummy with the king, and East plays the four. Which spade should you play?

STANLEY: The six, of course. I'll fool them both!

KANTAR: Correct. You have concealed the deuce from East, and furthermore, you might induce West to think that his partner is starting a signal from some such holding as Q 4 2. Had you played the deuce both defenders would have known what was going on immediately—by withholding it, you kept the count from East and raised doubts in the breast of West.

Now then, if West leads a four, you have two cards to look for, the trey and deuce. If you see both, you know West has a four-card suit; if you see one, West could have a five-card suit, and if you see neither, West could have a six-card suit.

DUMMY: ♠ A Q 7

WEST: ♠ K 10 5 4 3   EAST: ♠ 9 8

YOU: ♠ J 6 2

West leads the four and you can see the deuce, so you know that West started with no more than five spades. Later in the hand, if West plays the three, you know he started with five spades. If East, however, should drop the three, you'd know that West's original holding was four spades.

This is what experts do automatically every time a small card is led. Once, when I explained this to a class, a student asked, "Does that mean the Rule of Eleven doesn't work any more?"

It still works, but when a two, three, or four is led, it's easier to look for smaller spot cards than it is to subtract something from eleven. When the opening lead is a five, six, or seven, there are too many small cards to hunt, so use the Rule of Eleven.

DUMMY: ♠ A K 10

WEST LEADS: ♠ 6   EAST: ?

YOU: ♠ 9 8 3

West leads the six of spades against a notrump contract. You subtract six from eleven and with your usual brilliance come up with the correct answer, five. That means there are exactly five cards higher than the six in the three *remaining* hands. In this case there are three higher in dummy, and two higher in your hand—a total of five. That accounts for all the outstanding cards higher than the six in the *remaining* hands, so you can safely play the ten from dummy at trick one.

To help you see how this works, look at it from another angle: West has led the six and is known to hold three cards higher, since he's leading fourth best. There are only three cards higher than the six that you cannot see—the seven, jack, and queen. So naturally West figures to have them all and the ten will win the trick.

The Rule of Eleven will work any time an opponent leads a fourth best card, but if you see an eight on the table as an opening lead, watch out! An eight can be fourth highest from such holdings as A J 9 8, K J 9 8, or A Q 9 8, but many modern players holding five cards in a suit such as A J 9 8 3, prefer to lead the three rather than the honest fourth-best eight. The reason is that the eight is such a high card that leader's partner might think it's a bust lead from top of nothing.

To summarize: Look for the lower cards to get the count; conceal them to keep the count from your opponents; and remember the lead of a spot card usually shows three higher cards and possibly some lower if you can't see them. A high-low by the opening leader typically shows two or five cards, and the Rule of Eleven has not been repealed.

COUNT, COUNT, COUNT!

STANLEY: OK. But you must realize it's easier to theorize about these things than to apply them in practice. While working on this chapter, and thinking I knew it by heart, I ran into a hand that many duplicate players may have encountered in a Continent-wide Olympiad Fund Game:

East-West vulnerable
North dealer

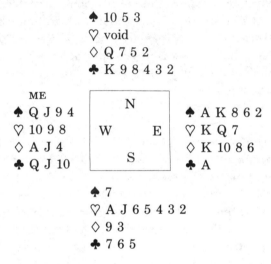

```
                      ♠ 10 5 3
                      ♡ void
                      ◇ Q 7 5 2
                      ♣ K 9 8 4 3 2

      ME                                    
      ♠ Q J 9 4         N          ♠ A K 8 6 2
      ♡ 10 9 8      W        E     ♡ K Q 7
      ◇ A J 4                      ◇ K 10 8 6
      ♣ Q J 10          S          ♣ A

                      ♠ 7
                      ♡ A J 6 5 4 3 2
                      ◇ 9 3
                      ♣ 7 6 5
```

The bidding:

NORTH	EAST	SOUTH	WEST (ME)
1 ♠ !!	Double	3 ♡	3 NT
All pass			

Our opponents were a pair of college students, playing a highly complicated system involving the use of controlled psychic bids. When it came my turn to call I was convinced we were being diddled, but had no way of showing it short of bidding three notrump. My partner had implied a tolerance for hearts by his double of one spade, so I knew we had a heart stop.

GAMESMAN BRIDGE

When the hand went down, we all had a good laugh. It was obvious to us all that they had conned us out of a spade game that everyone else would have bid. With everything right, a slam was by no means out of the question.

One of these days I'd better learn how to cope when the unusual arises in a bridge game. On this hand I should have realized that the opening psychic bid gave me a chance for a top on the board, for nobody else in the room would be playing notrump, which scores higher than spades. Instead, I played the hand in a state of mixed resignation and confusion. The opening lead was the four of clubs, taken by the ace. I came to hand with a spade, and started hearts. When North showed out, I knew South had seven, and that I was limited to a single heart trick.

South captured the king of hearts with the ace and returned a club, North ducking. I could now see ten tricks, and presuming that several pairs might have bid a slam on this hand, I elected to try to beat those who failed by playing safe. I ran the spades, came to my hand with the ace of diamonds, and refused the diamond finesse.

I was never quite able to get an accurate count on South's hand, but I see now I should have been concentrating on North. With a void in hearts and only three spades, he had to have ten minor suit cards—exactly twice as many as his partner. It was therefore a two-to-one proposition that he held the queen of diamonds. If I had taken that finesse, we'd have made a cold top, as everyone who bid the spade slam went down.

KANTAR: What good is all this stuff I give you, if you don't use it when the chips are down?

STANLEY: I remember the odds most of the time, but I often fail to relate them to the actual cards I hold.

KANTAR: In my classes, I try to demonstrate this visually. If, through counting, the declarer knows the opponents hold a queen in a suit distributed 4-2, it's easy to show that the odds are 2-to-1 for it to be in the hand holding four cards.

I ask my students to shuffle five spot-cards and a queen and deal them face down into two piles, one of four, and the other of two. When they turn the piles over, twice as many students find the queen in the four-pile as in the two-pile. I always get a laugh by telling them they can remember their odds if they remember their piles!

STANLEY: I guess in a bridge class a small amount of humor goes a long way.

KANTAR: If you can't develop a sense of humor, you'd better try another game. I was playing in a National Championship with Marshall Miles when I came up with this disconcerting hand. My opponents were Ken Barbour and Alan Truscott, bridge editor of the *New York Times*.

Neither vulnerable
West dealer

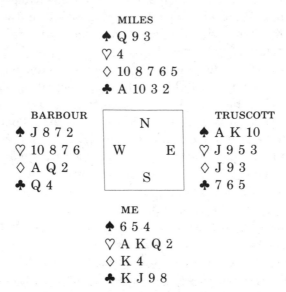

MILES
♠ Q 9 3
♡ 4
♢ 10 8 7 6 5
♣ A 10 3 2

BARBOUR
♠ J 8 7 2
♡ 10 8 7 6
♢ A Q 2
♣ Q 4

TRUSCOTT
♠ A K 10
♡ J 9 5 3
♢ J 9 3
♣ 7 6 5

ME
♠ 6 5 4
♡ A K Q 2
♢ K 4
♣ K J 9 8

GAMESMAN BRIDGE

The bidding:

WEST	NORTH	EAST	SOUTH
Pass	Pass	Pass	1 ♣
Pass	2 ♣	All pass	

We were playing weak notrumps (12-14) not vulnerable, so I couldn't open one notrump.

Ken led the deuce of spades, and Alan put in the ten, winning the trick. He followed with the ace and king of spades, switching to a small diamond. Since he had not opened the bidding, I knew the ace of diamonds was with West, so I played the four from my hand. West won the queen, continuing with the ace and a small diamond. I trumped in my hand and now faced the necessity of picking up the queen of trumps.

In keeping with an oft-repeated tenet of mine, *Put off your decisions on doubtful suits until the very end,* I played my ace, king, and queen of hearts, everyone following. (I discarded my established diamonds in the dummy.) Finally I led the deuce of hearts, and when West followed, I ruffed with the ten of clubs. This, in effect, was a finesse, because if Truscott was out of hearts, he needed the queen of clubs to overruff. But he followed with a heart, and my scheme paid off. I had a perfect count of the hand. East was 3-4-3-*3*, and West was 4-4-3-*2*. I've under-lined the distribution of the outstanding clubs, because that 3-2 represents the precise odds in favor of finding the queen of clubs with East. So finally, on the eleventh trick I decided to draw trumps.

You can see what happened. I finessed the jack of clubs and it lost to the *doubleton* queen. Down one.

STANLEY: So much for counting the hand. What's the next lesson, Master?

KANTAR: Show a little respect, please. And consider yourself lucky I haven't tried to teach you a system a friend of mine gave me for counting the hands. He said that when he was the declarer and the dummy came down he added the number of

COUNT, COUNT, COUNT!

spades he had in hand and dummy. Let's say it was five. This number he subtracted from thirteen to arrive at the number of spades held by his opponents, in this instance eight. He then repeated the process with the other suits to arrive at some four-digit figure such as 8549, representing the number of cards the opponents had started with in each of the four suits. He called this his telephone number.

Then, let's say a spade was led, all following. That meant his opponents had two fewer spades, so he changed his telephone number to 6549. After each trick he diminished each number accordingly.

STANLEY: Sounds gruesome. How did it work out?

KANTAR: I never bothered to find out, because then he started to tell me his system for remembering telephone numbers!

FIVE

The ever-never finesse

KANTAR: Now we return to the problem inspired by your father's recitation of that troublesome verse, "Eight ever, nine never." It rhymes, but that's about all it does. It oversimplifies a fairly complex problem, and for the lazy and indifferent, it is supposed to beat thinking. But it doesn't.

Created to answer the double-barreled question: If you have the ace and king of a suit, how do you capture the queen holding eight or nine cards in that suit? The doggerel suggests that you must finesse with eight and play to drop the queen with nine. Unfortunately, the advice works often enough to trap the innocent into giving up their right of self-determination. You're not only not obliged to follow the rhyme, but I'd strongly urge that you forget it altogether and start *thinking*.

In approaching the problem, we shall first consider the suit itself, and then regard the suit in relation to the rest of the hand. Obviously, the poet who wrote the verse paid no attention to the entire hand.

We'll start with a suit holding eight cards:

DUMMY: ♠ A 4 3 2

YOU: ♠ K 7 6 5

The trouble with this suit is that you're not only missing the queen but the jack and ten as well! There's no way you can pick up all three in two leads. You have two tricks guaranteed in the suit (assume you're playing notrump, or that this is your trump suit) and no amount of expert help will aid you in making more than three. If the opposing cards are split 3-2, you'll make your fourth small card; if they're split 4-1 you'll take only your ace and king.

Now let's try another combination:

DUMMY: ♡ A 4 3 2

'   YOU: ♡ K J 6 5

Ah, a big improvement. You are now in the market for four tricks in this suit, if the cards lie favorably.

With nothing else to go by you lead the ace and finesse the jack on the way back. What's so difficult about that? The nursery rhyme was right all the time. You have eight cards in the suit, so the finesse is "ever"—whatever that means.

But you forgot the words "with nothing else to go by." You forgot that this suit belongs in a hand. It doesn't exist in a vacuum, except here on the printed page. In real life it's in a hand with a bunch of other cards. And there's plenty else to go by! Not one hand in twenty exists "with nothing else to go by."

What if your left-hand opponent must not get the lead?
What if the queen is marked on your left from the bidding?

What if there is another finesse to take and you have a choice?

What if this is the trump suit and you need to ruff two losers in the dummy?

What if you are looking toward the end-game and want to throw the opponents in with that queen?

What if you have a count on the hand and you know your LHO has four cards in the suit?

What if a million things, none of which a miserable four-word verse can answer for you?

In order to play a suit properly it has to be put in a setting, and that setting is the hand. But before I give you some examples, I want to complicate your life a little by improving this suit again, stressing that if all other things are equal (they rarely are!) some ways of playing suits are better than others.

DUMMY: ♠ A J 3 2

YOU: ♠ K 10 5 4

With this combination your choice is widened. You can take the finesse to the left or the right, depending on some of the marvelous information you've picked up from the enemy. Has West shown up with most of the missing high cards in the hand? Has East discarded the suit? Has there been any informative bidding? But with no information at all, play either the ace or king—maybe you'll snare the queen!—and then finesse through the tenace opposite.

But what if your suit is even better?

DUMMY: ◇ A J 8 2

YOU: ◇ K 10 5 4

THE EVER-NEVER FINESSE

You have an eight in there, and now you can plot to save yourself from the bad luck of a 4-1 split. Up to now there was nothing you could do if one opponent held ◊ Q 9 7 6. Is that still true now that you have the eight in dummy? Is there a way you can pick up all four tricks?

The answer, of course, is negative if the ◊ Q 9 7 6 are with East. But if West has that holding, you'll have no trouble. Lay down the king, then lead the *ten*. West will be helpless. If he covers, win, and return to your hand in a side suit to finesse against the nine. That eight has suddenly become a mighty important card.

If the eight is in your hand, I shouldn't have to tell you what to do:

DUMMY: ◊ A J 3 2

YOU: ◊ K 10 8 5

Play the ace and then the jack, always remembering to play toward the hand with the greater number of broken intermediate cards. Don't forget, this is the best way to play this combination in the absence of other information.

DUMMY: ♡ K 4 3 2

YOU: ♡ A J 10 9

If your combination has improved to this point, you don't have to worry about the small cards—your only problem is to flush out that queen. With this holding you can handle four to the queen on either side, if you guess right. Perhaps you've counted the hand, so mere guessing is beneath you.

The artistic way to handle this suit is to lead the jack

toward the dummy. If your left-hand opponent doesn't cover with the queen or come up with a case of the shakes, rise with the king and finesse through your right-hand opponent.

DUMMY: ♣ K 9 3 2

YOU: ♣ A J 10 4

Be careful with this combination. It looks like the previous one, but you can't afford to overtake your jack on the occasions where the holding is ♣ Q 8 7 6 on your right. Play it out and you'll see that such wastefulness will cost you a trick. The only time you can afford to be so extravagant is when you're absolutely certain from the bidding or previous play that the suit is divided 3-2, or when you feel an opponent will make the common defensive error of covering an honor with an honor.

Up to now we've been discussing suits that are divided 4-4 between declarer and dummy. With 5-3 and 6-2 divisions you'll have further problems.

	a.	*b.*
DUMMY:	♣ A 3 2	◇ A 2
YOU:	♣ K J 6 5 4	◇ K J 6 5 4 3

	c.	*d.*
DUMMY:	♡ A 10 2	♠ A 10
YOU:	♡ K J 6 5 4	♠ K J 6 5 4 2

In examples *a* and *b* you have little choice. Lead the ace and finesse the jack. In *c* you can take the finesse either way, but again in *d* your choice is limited. Your best play is to go up with the ace in case the queen is a singleton, but if you believe West has the queen, you can always finesse the ten and hope East has at least a doubleton.

THE EVER-NEVER FINESSE

	e.	*f.*
DUMMY:	♠ 4 3 2	♡ 4 3
YOU:	♠ A K J 6 5	♡ A K J 7 6 5
	g.	*h.*
DUMMY:	◇ 4 3 2	♣ 4 3
YOU:	◇ A K J 10 9	♣ A K J 10 9 8

In all of these (except one!) you should place the ace on the table in hope of catching the singleton queen on your left. Failing this, enter dummy in a side suit and finesse the jack. Have you discovered the exception? In *e, f,* and *g* when you lay down the ace you're catering to the 2.8 percent of the time when the distribution is 4-1 with the queen singleton on your left. Taking advantage of a mere 2.8 percent doesn't sound like much of a saving, but if you live long enough it'll mount up in the end. In case *h,* however, you can pick up ♣ Q x x x on your right if you save your four and three in dummy to take two finesses. Since there's a greater chance of that holding than a singleton queen on your left, your best bet is to take two finesses.

I've made a big point of breaking down these card combinations, not because I expect you to memorize them, but because they demonstrate subtle differences you'll find in every hand you pick up. You'll find those same differences in the following.

	i	*j*
DUMMY:	♠ A 4 3 2	♡ A 10 4 3
YOU:	♠ K J 7 6 5	♡ K J 7 6 5
	k	*l*
DUMMY:	◇ A 10 8 2	♣ A 10 3 2
YOU:	◇ K J 5 4 3	♣ K J 8 5 4

Notice that you now have nine cards with ace-king, missing the elusive queen. I hate to say this, but on the rare occasions when you have nothing else to go by, you should play to drop the queen. But there's a right way and a wrong way to do it. You should insure yourself against bad breaks and take advantage of good ones.

In example *i* lead low to the ace and low to the king.

With *j* lead either the ace or king and then the ten or jack hoping to coax a cover. If there is no cover and no obvious case of indecision, rise with the high honor.

Now examine example *k*. Look at it carefully. Notice that eight? Well, since 10 percent of the time this suit will break tragically for you, 4-0, why not play the king first and if your right-hand opponent shows out you can forget the drop and go for the ironclad finesse against the Q 9 7 6? Half the 4-0 splits, of course, will be in the other direction, and with example *k* you can do nothing about those. That's when you ought to have example *l*, which I hope you will play by laying down the ace, taking out a small insurance policy by leaving the three-card K J 8 tenace available for finessing purposes.

Look at these two seemingly similar combinations.

	m	*n*
DUMMY:	♠ A 4 3 2	♡ A 4 3 2
YOU:	♠ K J 10 6 5	♡ K J 10 9 5

With example *m* lead low to the ace in case your right-hand opponent has four to the queen. Should you do the same thing with *n*? No, because you have a strong enough sequence to lead the jack toward the ace to see if your left-hand opponent is tempted to cover. If West shows out, go up with the ace and finesse twice against East's queen. (Try leading the jack with *m* and see what it gets you if East has all four missing cards!)

These combinations in which the queen is missing remind

THE EVER-NEVER FINESSE

me of the time when a pretty girl had vamped an expert into taking her on as his partner. She was not too successful in picking up pointers until the expert became declarer at a grand slam in hearts holding these cards:

	EXPERT			DUMMY
♠	7 6 2		♠	A K Q
♡	A K 10 9		♡	J 5 4 3
◇	A K J		◇	Q 7 6
♣	K 8 7 6		♣	A Q 2

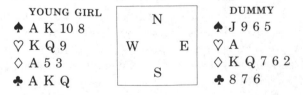

A club was led, and he won in his hand. He immediately played the ace of hearts and quickly followed that play with the king of *diamonds*. The combination of the heart ace followed by the diamond king was played so quickly that North thoughtlessly assumed the diamond king to be the heart king and "followed" with a small heart. Declarer cried out in mock dismay, and the North player saw in even greater dismay that she had revoked. Her small heart became an exposed card; it was then a simple matter for declarer to cross to the dummy with a spade and lead a heart through South, knowing he could take the finesse for the queen if necessary, since North was obliged to play the exposed card when the trick was led.

The pretty young girl was impressed with the expert's handling of this situation, and waited patiently for an opportunity to try it herself.

Her big moment came in a rubber bridge game some time later. She and her partner had bid up to seven spades, and she confronted this hand.

	YOUNG GIRL			DUMMY
♠	A K 10 8		♠	J 9 6 5
♡	K Q 9		♡	A
◇	A 5 3		◇	K Q 7 6 2
♣	A K Q		♣	8 7 6

GAMESMAN BRIDGE

The opening lead was a diamond, which she won in her hand. Displaying total recall, she put down the ace of trumps, followed quickly by the king of *clubs*. North followed to the first spade, and then played a small spade on the king of clubs. When the girl reminded him that she was playing clubs, not spades, he said, "I know. I don't have any."

So now we've covered advanced technique for finding the queen, let's look at some examples.

Neither vulnerable
South dealer

♠ K 10 5 2
♡ Q 7 3
◇ Q J 8 7
♣ K 3

YOU
♠ A J 7 6
♡ J 4 2
◇ A K 4 3
♣ A 4

The bidding:

SOUTH	NORTH
1 NT	2 ♣
2 ♠	4 ♠
All pass	

Opening Lead: queen of clubs.

THE EVER-NEVER FINESSE

The problem here is with an entire hand, not merely a troublesome suit. There are three losing hearts if you must lead them yourself, and if you misguess the trump finesse you're down!

What to do? Some people finesse toward East when the moon is full; hungry players finesse toward the kitchen; practical ones toward the ladies' room; and romanticists toward the boudoir.

But wait!

This time we have more than the mere suit to consider. We have the entire hand! Instead of throwing in the sponge, why not force the opponents to lead hearts for you, and forget the queen of spades!

You have eight cards in spades, but you should not take the finesse. Cash two rounds of spades. If the queen doesn't drop, cash your club and diamond winners in that order. If someone ruffs a diamond, that someone will be obligated to play hearts or give you a ruff-sluff. Either way it's money in the bank. You can't lose more than three tricks.

Tip: When you wish opponents to play a particular side suit to you, it often pays to abandon finesses in trumps and use the missing trump honor for the throw-in. This play usually requires at least one trump remaining in hand and dummy at the time you pass the buck to your adversaries.

Bonus tip: If you are compulsive and finesse for the queen with this hand, losing it, you may still have a chance to win a trick holding ♡ Q 7 3 in one hand and ♡ J 4 2 in the other. Besides, a throw-in is sometimes possible, and you ought to learn to tackle this combination yourself. Here are the most commons situations.

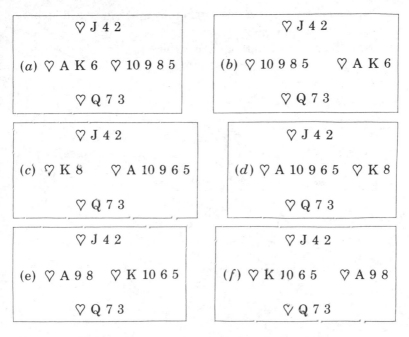

If you think both honors are in one hand, as in examples *a* and *b*, simply remember to lead first from one hand and then from the other. It won't matter which side has both honors or from which hand you lead first—you always win one trick. Try it and see.

Cases *c* and *d* are a little more difficult. If you think the honors are split and have reason to believe the adverse distribution is 5-2, simply remember to lead *through* the hand with the doubleton (from your hand in *c* and from the board in (*d*) and, next time you're in, play small from both hands, crashing the king on air.

In cases *e* and *f* there's no way against best defense. However playing the jack from the dummy (f) works against relatives or close friends who duck with the ace or king. Later you can lead from dummy towards your other honor.

THE EVER-NEVER FINESSE

Super bonus tip: Avoid putting yourself in a spot where you have to use the bonus tip.

Now then, see if you can solve this one.

Neither vulnerable.
West dealer

♠ 8 7 6
♡ A Q J 5
◇ 4 3
♣ 8 7 6 5

YOU
♠ A K J 10 9
♡ 6 2
◇ K J 6
♣ K 4 3

The bidding:

WEST	NORTH	EAST	SOUTH
1 ◇	Pass	Pass	2 ♠
Pass	3 ♠	All pass	

West, who opened the bidding, led the five of diamonds. His passing partner won with the ace to return the jack of clubs. You ducked, and he continued a club. You ducked again, showing none of your normal anxiety. West won with the queen and cashed his ace. He now exited with a small heart. Now that you've lost four tricks, how do you bring in all the rest?

GAMESMAN BRIDGE

STANLEY: Since West opened the bidding, he's marked with the heart king. That one I finesse. I have eight cards in spades missing the queen which I suspect lies with West, also.

KANTAR: You don't suspect, you know! East passed an opening bid of one diamond and has already shown the ace of diamonds and jack of clubs. Is there a chance in the world of his holding the queen of spades for a total of seven high-card points and not keeping the bidding open? So long as you know West has the queen of spades, you have no alternative but to play off the ace and king of spades, hoping for a fortuitous drop. Pay strict attention during the play to the high-card holding of opponents who have limited their hands:

1. West—1 ♥ East—Pass. East has 5 points or fewer.
2. West—1 ♥ East—1 NT East has 6-9 points.
3. West—1 NT East—? Whenever West becomes declarer it is easy to assess his strength within three points as long as you know whether he plays strong (16-18), weak (12-14), or middling (15-17) notrumps. Typically you will know his distribution after a few cards have been played. It should be 4-3-3-3, 4-4-3-2, or 5-3-3-2.

When the bidding marks a player with a particular card, play him for the card in spite of the "technically correct" way to play the suit.

Both vulnerable
South dealer

♠ 9 6
♡ K 4 3
◇ A K J 10 5
♣ K 8 5

YOU
♠ K 5
♡ A J 7 2
◇ 6 4 3
♣ A Q 3 2

The bidding:

SOUTH	NORTH
1 ♣	1 ◇
1 NT	3 NT
All pass	

Opening lead: four of spades.

East wins the ace of spades and returns the deuce. You win the king, West playing the three. How do you play the diamonds?

STANLEY: I guess first the ace—

KANTAR: Don't be distracted by these direct questions! This lesson concerns the entire hand! Look at it. You have eight top tricks, plus a ninth in case the clubs divide 3-3. So go for the clubs first. OK, let's assume everything is normal and they divide against your deepest desires, 4-2. Now at last you may go for the diamonds, but *play for the drop!* If you don't catch the queen, you have one more shot in your arquebus. Play the king of hearts and then finesse the jack.

So there you are, right back where you started, faced with a 50 percent chance to make your contract. But on the way, you've taken advantage of other possibilities to give yourself the irreducible maximum for success, 79 percent.*

General tip: Go through a hand like it was a rummage sale. Try everything on before you buy.

Specific Tip: With two finesses to take, either of which will give you your contract, play the ace-king of the longer suit, and if the queen doesn't fall, finesse in the shorter suit.

---

*It's interesting the way mathematicians figure this out. It doesn't matter which alternative you start with but, for instance, let's take it in the order above. The club division of 3-3 is a 36 percent chance. If it fails, your base is now (100 minus 36) = 64 percent. To drop the queen of diamonds is 33 percent *of 64 percent,* or roughly 21 percent. If that fails, your new base will be (64 minus 21) = 43 percent. Now your finesse for the king of hearts is 50 percent *of 43 percent or* 21 + percent. Add up all the favorable percents—36 percent, 21 percent, and 21 + percent—and you'll come close enough to 79 percent even for a mathematician.

Both vulnerable
South dealer

♠ K 6 5 4
♡ A 6 5 4
◇ 8 3
♣ K 6 5

♠ A 7 3
♡ K 8
◇ A 10 6
♣ A J 4 3 2

The bidding:

SOUTH	NORTH
1 NT	2 ♣
2 ◇	3 NT
All pass	

West opened the four of diamonds. East played the king and you refused the trick. He returned the jack, and you ducked again. West overtook with the queen, and continued the suit. East followed with the five, and you finally had to play your ace. How are you planning to play your clubs?

STANLEY: I'm getting smart. West started with five diamonds, so I must play for a drop with the ace-king of clubs.

KANTAR: That's right. You can't afford to finesse into the danger hand. The technically correct way to play this combination is to lead small toward the king in dummy and if West holds something like ♣ Q 10 7 and slips up by playing the seven, you can duck and East will be forced to overtake. If West

GAMESMAN BRIDGE

plays any other card, you must go up and come back hoping to drop the queen. If it doesn't drop but East has it, you're still safe.

Tip: When the only suit you can establish has a one-way finesse for the queen headed straight into the danger hand, play the ace-king and then a third round so as not to lose to a doubleton queen in the danger hand. (This presumes, of course, that the partner of the danger hand cannot hurt you if he gets the lead. If both hands are dangerous, close your eyes and take the finesse!)

East-West vulnerable
West dealer

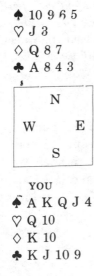

♠ 10 9 6 5
♡ J 3
◇ Q 8 7
♣ A 8 4 3

YOU
♠ A K Q J 4
♡ Q 10
◇ K 10
♣ K J 10 9

The bidding:

WEST	NORTH	EAST	SOUTH (YOU)
2 ♡*	Pass	Pass	3 ♠
Pass	4 ♠	All pass	

*Weak two-bid.

THE EVER-NEVER FINESSE

West opened the king of hearts, followed by the ace, his partner signaling low-high. West shifted to the nine of diamonds, won by East with the ace. East hopefully returned a diamond, which you captured with the king. You played three rounds of spades, ending in dummy. West had one and East three. How do you play the clubs?

STANLEY: Maybe I should have ended in my own hand, played the jack of clubs and if West didn't cover, gone up with the ace and finessed on the way back.

KANTAR: That's the way to play the *suit*. But this is a *hand*. I thought I'd make it easy for you by leaving you in dummy. The correct way to play those clubs is to continue with diamonds.

Repeat tip: Any time you can lead a safe card in a side suit to give you a count on the hand, do so!

In this hand, if you lead the queen of diamonds from the board, you'll discover that West is void!

His opening bid suggested six hearts, and he had one spade. He now shows up with only two diamonds. How many clubs, Archimedes?

STANLEY: Don't rush me. Four.

KANTAR: Good! So come to your hand with the king of clubs, and lead your jack through West.

Now let's look at a hand which should be played two different ways, depending on how it is bid.

Both vulnerable
South dealer

♠ K 7 6
♡ 5 4
◊ 10 9 8
♣ A K J 10 9

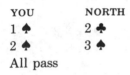

YOU
♠ A J 10 3 2
♡ A J 3
◊ 7 6 2
♣ Q 4

The bidding:

YOU	NORTH
1 ♠	2 ♣
2 ♠	3 ♠
All pass	

West started out with the king and queen of diamonds, followed by a third diamond to East's jack. East shifted to a low heart. You went in with your ace. How should you play your trump suit?

STANLEY: Prayerfully.

KANTAR: This is not a theological problem. Don't give up hope. You have two chances. Play off your ace and king of spades. You might drop the queen. If not, start the clubs. If the queen of spades lies in the hand containing three or more clubs, you're safe. You can discard your two hearts on clubs, losing only three diamonds and one spade.

THE EVER-NEVER FINESSE

But consider the way you would play the same hand if it were bid this way:

YOU	NORTH
1 ♠	2 ♣
2 ♠	4 ♠
All pass	

The lead is the same, and on the fourth trick you find yourself in hand with the ace of hearts. I won't ask what you should do, because it's obvious. You must take the rest of the tricks. So play a spade to the king and a spade to the jack. If the finesse loses, you're down two; but if it works, you can spread the hand.

The difference between these two situations ought to be clear. If not, study them. When your contract is at stake, don't play for down one!

Here's one that's easy.

Neither vulnerable
North dealer

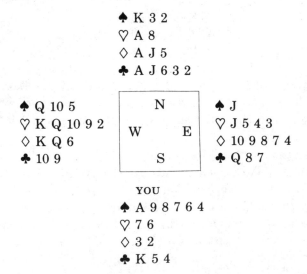

```
                    ♠ K 3 2
                    ♡ A 8
                    ◇ A J 5
                    ♣ A J 6 3 2

  ♠ Q 10 5          ┌─────────┐          ♠ J
  ♡ K Q 10 9 2      │    N    │          ♡ J 5 4 3
  ◇ K Q 6           │ W     E │          ◇ 10 9 8 7 4
  ♣ 10 9            │    S    │          ♣ Q 8 7
                    └─────────┘
                      YOU
                    ♠ A 9 8 7 6 4
                    ♡ 7 6
                    ◇ 3 2
                    ♣ K 5 4
```

GAMESMAN BRIDGE

The bidding:

NORTH	SOUTH
1 ♣	1 ♠
2 ♠	4 ♠
All pass	

West leads the king of hearts.

STANLEY: I can see myself losing a trick in each suit, the mean, contemptible way you've laid out the cards. I'll take the ace of hearts and start trumps, learning that West sits safely with the winning queen. Then I'll try the club finesse, hoping to set up the suit for losing diamond and heart discards. No dice, Svengali, you've stacked the deck and I'm down one.

KANTAR: Hold on. Once you've discovered the bad trump break, your problems are over if West has at least two clubs, and you can resist the temptation to foolishly finesse the suit.

After the trump plays, cash the ace-king and give up a club. Your opponents will grab their heart trick and knock out your diamond ace, but you'll be in control. Simply play an established club and discard your losing diamond. You lose three tricks, a trump, a club, and a heart.

The plan in this hand is to set up the clubs in such a way that you lose a third-round trick rather than a second. The way you played it, after you lost the second-round finesse, the opponents cashed their heart and shifted to a diamond *while they still had a trump control.* When you led to your established clubs, West trumped and grabbed the setting diamond trick before you could dispose of it.

So now we've seen a bunch of eight-card suits arranged in hands that do not recommend themselves to poetry reading. How much versification can we stand if we hold nine cards to the ace-king, missing the queen?

Very little, if the verse is "Eight ever, nine never."

Both vulnerable
North dealer

        ♠ K 9 5 3
        ♡ 7 5 3
        ◇ A Q 10 6
        ♣ A 2

        YOU
        ♠ A J 10 8 7
        ♡ K 4 2
        ◇ K J 7
        ♣ K 3

The bidding:

NORTH	SOUTH
1 ◇	1 ♠
2 ♠	4 ♠
All pass	

Opening lead: queen of clubs.

    This is a textbook hand, used so often in newspaper columns that I'm not sure whether I stole it from another column or somebody stole it from me. In any case, here it is, stolen right back.

    You don't have to look at it very hard to see the problem. If you plunk down the ace-king of trumps, you may find East with the protected queen. As soon as he gets in, perhaps ruffing the third round of diamonds, he'll lead through your king of hearts, and you know where you always find the ace-queen in the newspapers—hovering over the king!

This hand is childishly safe if you haven't been corrupted by the poetic fallacy. Plunk down nothing. Instead of charging into the valley of death, finesse into the non-danger hand. You don't really care if West has the doubleton queen of spades. Lead to the king and finesse on the way back. If West wins, there will be no heart lead through your king until after you have discarded a heart on your fourth diamond. The problem isn't whether or not to take the finesse, but rather to keep East out of the lead.

Now, what if this were your spade holding in that same hand?

NORTH: ♠ K 4 3 2

YOU: ♠ A 10 9 8 6

You'd lead to the king and if an honor dropped from West you should finesse the ten on the way back. You might lose to the doubleton queen-jack, but you would make your contract, as you are perfectly willing for West to take the trick. One heart discard assures you of the contract.

This very combination produced a spectacular result in a recent tournament. Declarer, playing a grand slam in spades, led the ten and West covered with the jack. The trick was won by the king in dummy, and then declarer went into a trance trying to decide whether to play for the drop or take the finesse.

As he was thinking, East immortalized himself by asking, "Partner, did you play the queen or the jack?"

Here's a final example illustrating an old principle:

Both vulnerable
North dealer

♠ A J 8
♡ A 10 3 2
◇ A K 5
♣ 7 6 5

YOU
♠ K 10 7 6 5 4
♡ K J 9
◇ 7 3
♣ 8 4

The bidding:

NORTH	EAST	SOUTH	WEST
1 NT	Pass	4 ♠	All pass

West opened the king of clubs followed by the ace and a small club to East's jack which you were smart enough to ruff. Now what?

STANLEY: I guess this is the finesse lesson.

KANTAR: You guess right, but you guess too soon. Play off the ace-king of diamonds and ruff a diamond in your hand. Now lead a spade to the ace, then lead the jack. Assume East follows with a small spade. What do you do?

STANLEY: I stick by my guns!

KANTAR: I guess by that you mean to take the finesse.

That's correct, for if it loses, West will be end-played and forced to lead hearts or give you a ruff-sluff. If the finesse works, you can fish around for an overtrick by guessing the hearts correctly.

If East fails to follow suit when you lead the jack of spades, you know that West holds the guarded queen. It won't do you any good to lose to the queen, as West can escape the end-play by getting out with his small trump. You still have a fighting chance, however, if you go up with your king and throw West in with his queen. West may be out of clubs and diamonds and be forced to lead hearts. If he still has a card in the minors, you'll be forced to guess the heart yourself. In any event, remember this: Holding nine cards does not automatically call for an attempt to drop the queen.

Forget those nursery rhymes!

SIX

Lead, as in bleed

STANLEY: I've often felt that what brought my father to an early grave was the anxiety he suffered in waiting for his partner's opening lead.

He claimed he had never seen me make one that didn't give a trick to the declarer. He was close to the truth, of course, for after a hand is over it's much easier to achieve the perfection that only precognition promises.

My father was never quite able to convince me that it is easy to decide whether to make a passive or an active lead against suit contracts. Half the time he grumbled because I didn't lead a trump to shorten dummy's ruffing power, and the other time he was bellowing that I should have established our winners before declarer was able to set up his side suit.

As a result, when it was my turn to lead, he squirmed in his chair as though somebody was twisting a piano wire round his neck.

I remember once when we were playing against two girls. In other circumstances, my father was the soul of gallantry, but as soon as a woman picked up thirteen cards she renounced all the rights and privileges usually accorded what before Women's Lib we referred to as "the weaker sex." My father believed that the adjective was well chosen to describe the average woman's ability at the bridge table. He expected his partners to be imaginative, aggressive, and decisive. Most women when playing with him were generally bullied into a state where terror, vacillation, and frozen-mindedness were their chief adornments.

As my father's opponents, however, women showed remarkable resourcefulness. Perhaps it was sheer relief at not having cut him as partner. From the other side of the table they took on a measure of wisdom he rarely associated with the human female, and he afforded his partners a special larding of wrath when their bad play enabled women opponents to win. Winning deceived them as to their ability, rendering them skeptical of the advice he so freely delivered them.

This particular hand not only resulted in painfully eroding any idea I might have had as to the supremacy of the male, but it contributed to a lifelong confusion as to the proper time to lead trumps.

Both vulnerable
South dealer

FIRST WOMAN

♠ J 4 2
♡ 10 3
◊ 8 4 2
♣ A K Q 8 7

ME		MY FATHER
♠ 10 8 6	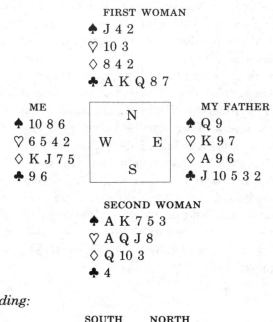	♠ Q 9
♡ 6 5 4 2		♡ K 9 7
◊ K J 7 5		◊ A 9 6
♣ 9 6		♣ J 10 5 3 2

SECOND WOMAN

♠ A K 7 5 3
♡ A Q J 8
◊ Q 10 3
♣ 4

The bidding:

SOUTH	NORTH
1 ♠	2 ♣
2 ♡	2 ♠
4 ♠	All pass

When the bidding was over, everyone turned to me for the lead, and I subsided into one of those trances that so often contributed to my father's rising blood pressure. I fingered several cards with varying degrees of interest in them. The nine of clubs teased me, as it would be leading through dummy's strength. I pushed the five of diamonds away like a hot potato, shuddering at the thought of leading from a king-jack. I lingered hardly at all on the heart suit, as a lead *up* to strength might put my father into a coma. Running out of rope, I finally led a trump, enjoying some vague hope that it could reduce dummy's ruffing power.

GAMESMAN BRIDGE

Declarer looked briefly at my six of spades on the table and was off like a shot. I don't know what got into that girl, but she played the hand like winning was everything. She pulled trumps, tossed two of her losing diamonds on dummy's clubs, finessed the heart, and made six-odd.

My father's reaction was overly dramatic, even for him. While writing down the score, he broke the pencil and threw the stub across the room. The sound that came from his throat was like somebody had stabbed the parrot. When he could speak without spluttering, he roared in anguish, "How could you be so stupid! Couldn't you see you had to get *busy* on this hand?"

"Y—you mean lead from the king-jack of diamonds?"

"What else, what else, with them bidding the other three suits!"

I mumbled something in apology, and then trucked out that tired old saw, "Anyway, they'd still have made their contract."

My father's retort to that was tight-lipped. "Of course, because even if you'd won three diamond tricks, you'd be too dumb to see the way to set them."

The declarer, never too fearful to argue with my father as long as she didn't have to play with him, insisted she could have made ten tricks even if I had opened a diamond.

My father corrected her with lordly condescension. "If my idiot son had led a fourth diamond, I could have trumped and promoted his ten of trumps for a trick whether you decided to ruff in dummy or in your hand!"

The agitation was too great for my poor father. He begged off for the rest of the afternoon, the victim of a nagging headache. The way he looked at me I knew he was gazing darkly into the future. What would happen to this great country of ours when imbeciles like me were let loose to take charge?

I suppose the lesson was good for me, because I have been a fairly aggressive leader ever since. But then along came this hand, also against feminine opponents, and I blew it again.

♠ J 10 3   ♡ J 3   ◇ Q J 9 3   ♣ K J 7 4

I was sitting West in a nearby sectional and the opposition reached game after the following auction:

NORTH	SOUTH
1 ♣	1 ♡
1 ♠	2 ♡
3 ♣	3 ♡
4 ♡	All pass

What should I lead?

The bidding sounded suspiciously nervous, and I thought I ought to be able to set the hand. South was an excellent player who had bid her suit three times with relentless precision. Her partner was a beginner who could best be trusted only when she was dummy. She had found increasing difficulty with each of her bids, until when she bid four hearts, South uttered an involuntary gasp of despair.

My table manners are usually impeccable, but I laughed before making my lead. It was the queen of diamonds, and when you see the hand, we'll all have a laugh.

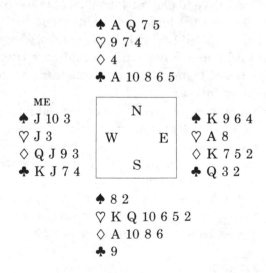

```
                    ♠ A Q 7 5
                    ♡ 9 7 4
                    ◇ 4
                    ♣ A 10 8 6 5
      ME                 N
      ♠ J 10 3                      ♠ K 9 6 4
      ♡ J 3          W        E     ♡ A 8
      ◇ Q J 9 3                     ◇ K 7 5 2
      ♣ K J 7 4          S          ♣ Q 3 2
                    ♠ 8 2
                    ♡ K Q 10 6 5 2
                    ◇ A 10 8 6
                    ♣ 9
```

GAMESMAN BRIDGE

They might have taken some time to arrive at the contract, but South took her first eight tricks in a blinding minor suit cross-ruff, ending with a club from dummy. My partner was so agitated by my play that he trumped dummy's fourth club with the eight in the hopes of promoting one of mine! South overruffed and put down the king of hearts, neatly forcing my partner to lead up to her spades on the board.

"Five!" cried South in some surprise. With a sweet smile she paid me back for my laugh. "I think you'd have murdered me with a trump lead," she said.

"Bidding called for it," snapped my partner, cleverly shifting the blame onto me for the end-play.

So here I am, ignorant and half-clothed, a savage lumbering about in a civilized land. How do I know whether to lead trumps or not?

KANTAR: Generally speaking, leading trumps is a bit over-rated, working well when called for, but otherwise like starting a campfire with high octane gasoline.

If you want to see an example of the hideous punishment reserved for people who lead trumps, look what happened when I was playing in the Summer Nationals in Boston in the Life Masters Pairs with a pupil of mine, Mrs. Paul Shearer.

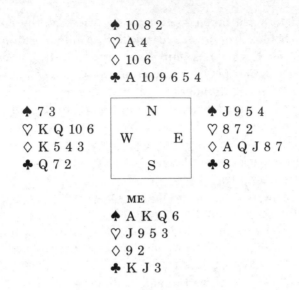

♠ 10 8 2
♡ A 4
◇ 10 6
♣ A 10 9 6 5 4

♠ 7 3
♡ K Q 10 6
◇ K 5 4 3
♣ Q 7 2

N
W   E
S

♠ J 9 5 4
♡ 8 7 2
◇ A Q J 8 7
♣ 8

ME
♠ A K Q 6
♡ J 9 5 3
◇ 9 2
♣ K J 3

The bidding:
East dealer

SOUTH	NORTH
1 ♠	3 ♠
4 ♠	All pass

Had West made the normal lead of the king of hearts, I would certainly have gone down—what with the bad breaks in the black suits.

Instead, West led his three of trumps, covered by the eight, nine, and my king. I then led the ace of spades, and noting the fall of West's seven, unblocked dummy's ten. Since a player who leads trump usually has honors in the other suits, I led a low club and finessed dummy's nine. I then led the deuce of trumps from the table and finessed the six. When it held, I drew the last trump and ran off the clubs to make eleven tricks!

Referring to that cross-ruff hand you mentioned—did you listen to the bidding? You should suspect that when a beginning player opens a club and then bids spades she *always* rebids her clubs if she's 5-4 so her partner won't think she's on a "short club"? Consequently, after South signed off at three hearts, North felt she had to bid four because she'd been hoarding three trumps she hadn't had time to mention! You knew she had three, because she'd be terrified of raising on two, no matter how many times her partner had bid the suit.

Therefore, how many diamonds could she have held? Her 5-4 in the black suits and three hearts make your diamond lead an outstanding *negative*. This is one of those rare occasions when you should lead a trump. I'd have picked the jack, in case your guess about the three trumps in dummy was wrong. If your partner held something like Q x x, declarer wouldn't be able to finesse it if he had to ruff a diamond in dummy.

As the cards lay, your partner would have taken the ace of trumps and returned the suit. Later you couldn't be prevented from taking two diamonds and a spade.

STANLEY: Yes, yes, I've already been through that with my partner. I'm tired of hearing about what I *should* have done. What I want from you is some kind of clue to keep me out of trouble in the *future*.

KANTAR: If I happen to tell you, be sure to return the favor! I not only can't prevent you from making bad leads from time to time, I can't prevent *me* from making them. But at least I have enough experience to keep me out of trouble most of the time.

STANLEY: A good thing it is, too. Can you imagine a bridge teacher leading as badly as I do?

KANTAR: Yes, but only in a nightmare. Meanwhile, I keep reminding myself that signs of sudden brilliance in students is always possible.

Just as you have learned that no suit exists in a vacuum, that it must be considered in relationship to the entire hand, so you must consider each hand in relationship to the other three. This is difficult enough when you're declarer, quite difficult when you're defending, but most difficult of all when you're on lead. It's a partnership game and you expect your partner's hand to augment your own, but you often haven't a clue as to what he holds. Furthermore you haven't seen the dummy, so you're at a point of maximum ignorance. All you have to go by is:

1. Your own thirteen cards.
2. The bidding.
3. What your partner *hasn't* bid.

Now everyone knows that it's quite possible for a perfectly respectable lead to go sour, but that mustn't discourage you, because according to the rules of the game, you have to lead *something*. And if you've listened to the bidding and lead the correct card in the suit you choose to lead, I think you shouldn't embarrass yourself more than one time in fifteen leads.

During the bidding you should use your time wisely in case your right-hand opponent lands the contract. Then, it being your lead, you should have the answers to these key questions:

1. Has your pàrtner bid? If he has, your problems are few, particularly if he has overcalled, since such a bid usually shows a good suit.

2. Does dummy have a long strong suit upon which declarer can shed losers? You can't always be sure dummy's suit is long or strong unless he rebids it. If you hold K x x or Q x x in dummy's suit, you can guarantee that it's much stronger than declarer will think it is at first glance! If you have four or five of dummy's suit and not many trumps, you can live in hope that partner's ruffs will prevent discards for declarer.

3. Does dummy have a short suit? This is often difficult to divine. Dummy can't very well bid two suits and ultimately support declarer without showing up with a short suit. When dummy makes a choice of declarer's two suits, he suggests shortness in the one he refused. When dummy corrects three notrump to game in a suit, you can suspect a shortness in something other than his breath.

4. *Do either you or your partner hold four trumps?* You can easily tell whether or not you hold four by looking at your hand. That also happens to be the way you estimate partner to have four. Certain bidding sequences lend themselves to an easy count. One spade–two clubs–two diamonds–two spades is almost certain to show a 5-3 fit in spades. If you hold one spade, a genius like you should be able to work out partner's trump length.

5. *Do you hold trump control, either ace or king, with one or two small trumps?* Look carefully for A x or K x x in trumps, holdings which lend themselves to short suit leads.

6. *Do you have a comfortable honor sequence?* Holding queen-jack-ten beats thinking for a lazy leader. Best of all, of course, are suits headed by the ace-king. With them, it's often possible to make a lead while mixing a drink, watching a ball game, and answering the front door!

7. *Do you have a hunch?* Have your opponents failed to bid a certain suit, or have they shied away from notrump? Have their bids been hesitant or full of confidence? Have some of their bids sounded unnatural to you, suggesting they're trying to inhibit a lead in some suit? Give a little thought to an enemy cue bid of a suit bid by you or partner; not only is there no law that your opponents must have an honest first-round control, but many players now make enemy suit cue bids to *ask* if partner has a partial control or a full stopper. Have they arrived at game briskly, or was it pull-and-tug all the way? In other words keep your ears open.

Now that you've asked yourself a fistful of questions and come up with all the answers, you probably still don't know what to do. Patience.

1. As I hinted before, if your partner has bid a suit (particularly as an overcall), it's usually reasonable, if not best, to lead his suit. (For a notable exception, see paragraph 5 below.) I can remember many times when I haven't led partner's suit,

but never without having prepared a good excuse. Holding ♡ A x x over declarer who has previously bid notrump over partner's heart bid may be cause for you to lead some other suit, but much depends on the level at which partner has bid and upon other factors (e.g., do you have to cash out your tricks quickly?).

When it comes to which *card* to lead in partner's suit, my advice is: With any two cards lead the higher, and with three or four small cards lead the lowest *unless you have supported partner* (implying three or four), in which case you should lead the highest.

This is very important. For example, if you have something like the 8 6 3 in partner's suit, lead the three if you haven't supported his suit; but lead the eight if you have. If you follow this advice, declarer will not be able to falsecard effectively and partner will know if you have led from shortness or length and will be able to plan the defense accordingly.

Neither vulnerable
North dealer

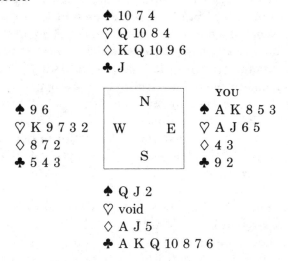

GAMESMAN BRIDGE

The bidding:

NORTH	EAST	SOUTH	WEST
Pass	1 ♠	5 ♣	All pass

Opening lead: nine of spades.

If you and partner are leading top in partner's suit, sitting East you will have a nasty decision to make at trick three. If you cash your two spades, South will naturally falsecard by dropping the queen and the jack, retaining the deuce. Believing partner may have started with ♠ 9 6 2, your proper play will be to cash the ace of hearts before it goes away on the diamonds.

However, if you know that partner would lead the deuce from the ♠ 9 6 2, you know that declarer is teasing you with his play of the queen-jack and you can set the contract by leading a third spade for partner to ruff.

If you decide to lead partner's suit when holding the ace, you should lead the ace against a suit contract, but lead low holding three or more cards against a notrump contract. (If you have two touching honors—say, K Q x x or Q J x x—you should lead your highest card.)

I know how automatic it is for some people to lead the highest of partner's suit, but unless you're willing to lose an astronomical number of points in the long run, don't do it! Holding three or four to one honor in partner's suit, it is almost always right to lead low, with two notable exceptions:

a. When the dummy to your left has bid notrump and your partner has overcalled, lead your honor through the honor you presume dummy holds.

b. When holding four or five cards to the king and no outside picture cards, it often pays to lead the king. Since it will probably hold the trick, you can use this opportunity, undoubtedly your last, either to continue partner's suit or lead through some strength in dummy. Your partner's signal and the appearance of dummy will aid you in making this decision.

There is a third exception which I learned in one of my classes. An elderly lady stood up and announced that no matter what I said, she was going to continue leading the highest card in her partner's suit. Otherwise, she said firmly, her lady friends wouldn't play with her any more!

2. If you decide that dummy has a long strong suit, you have no alternative but to get busy before declarer sheds his losers. This is when you should lead from kings and queens, hoping to find partner with adjacent honors that can be established before dummy's suit sets up.

Given the choice among three suits headed by a king, a queen, or a jack, experts will most often lead from the king. It's by far the safest choice. If you lead from a king, you will gain if partner has the ace or queen and may break even if he only has the jack. In other words, you only have to find one honor in partner's hand. But if you lead from an unsupported jack, it will almost always cost you a trick unless partner holds two honors. Most other choices are preferable to leading from the jack.

Inexperienced players who finally lead from a king— sometimes fall apart when their suit is improved by the addition of a jack (K J x x). A lead from this holding is actually better than one from the unsupported king. If the opponents held the ace and queen between them, they might have bid notrump somewhere along the line.

Experts shy away from making an attacking lead in a suit in which they hold the ace. This deal exemplifies expert thinking on the subject of opening leads.

Both vulnerable
South dealer

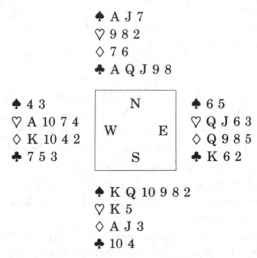

♠ A J 7
♡ 9 8 2
◇ 7 6
♣ A Q J 9 8

♠ 4 3   N   ♠ 6 5
♡ A 10 7 4   ♡ Q J 6 3
◇ K 10 4 2   W   E   ◇ Q 9 8 5
♣ 7 5 3   S   ♣ K 6 2

♠ K Q 10 9 8 2
♡ K 5
◇ A J 3
♣ 10 4

The bidding.

SOUTH	NORTH
1 ♠	2 ♣
2 ♠	4 ♠
All pass	

West's lead of the deuce of diamonds should be automatic. Clubs and spades are out since either one may give declarer valuable time to establish the probable long club suit on the table. Since it is far safer to lead from a king than an ace, (you don't want to lose a trick to declarer's king!) West really has no second choice.

South wins the ace of diamonds, draws two rounds of trump ending in his own hand, and runs the ten of clubs. East wins the king and realizes that the defense can pick up no more than one trick in diamonds because of dummy's original doubleton in that suit. Two heart tricks are obviously needed to defeat the contract. East shifts to the queen of hearts and declarer must lose two hearts, a club, and a diamond.

LEAD, AS IN BLEED   85

3. If dummy has a short suit but no long strong one, and if the bidding indicates that declarer would like to use dummy's trumps to take care of losers in his own hand, you should consider a trump lead. When you have some high cards in declarer's first-bid suit, you're entitled to try to prevent declarer from ruffing them in dummy. Bidding such as one spade–one no-trump–two hearts–pass suggests a singleton spade in dummy. A trump is often the best lead, particularly if you have good spades. If, in addition, you have length and strength in dummy's long suit and have reason to believe partner has length and strength in declarer's second suit (because you are short), it sometimes pays to lead trumps to prevent a cross-ruff. Another time to lead trumps is when you have made a takeout double and partner has passed, announcing that he has length and strength in declarer's suit.

Except in the last case, when it's not impossible that partner has more trumps than declarer, it's rarely wise to lead a singleton trump. Seldom do you ever lead trumps from four, preferring a forcing game by leading from your longest suit to chop declarer down to your size—or smaller!

When you do lead trumps, it's best to lead small, since it's not unheard of for the ten in 10 x x to be promoted to a trick, even after you've led one.

Finally, don't lead trumps because you're "in doubt." When in doubt about what to lead, my advice is to lead anything *but* trumps. The best time to lead trumps is when you know exactly why you're leading them!

4. If either you or partner have four trumps and declarer bids as if he has four or five, it is time to launch a forcing game. Lead your longest suit, or perhaps partner's suit if he has bid one. The idea is to force declarer to trump. If you force him often enough he may lose control of the hand. Your side's fourth trump may become the master trump.

Take a look at this example of the forcing game.

Neither vulnerable
South dealer

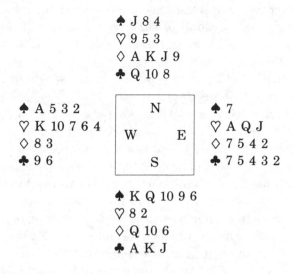

♠ J 8 4
♡ 9 5 3
◇ A K J 9
♣ Q 10 8

♠ A 5 3 2
♡ K 10 7 6 4
◇ 8 3
♣ 9 6

N
W E
S

♠ 7
♡ A Q J
◇ 7 5 4 2
♣ 7 5 4 3 2

♠ K Q 10 9 6
♡ 8 2
◇ Q 10 6
♣ A K J

The bidding:

SOUTH	NORTH
1 ♠	2 ◇
3 ◇	3 ♠
4 ♠	All pass

An inexperienced player, thinking in terms of ruffing, might lead the nine of clubs on this bidding, but an expert would have the six of hearts on the table simultaneously with the last "pass." He can tell from the bidding that spades are 5-3 and with his own holding of four trumps he is intent on forcing declarer. Watch how it works—when it works.

The defenders play three rounds of hearts, South trumping. South tries to knock out the ace of spades, but West ducks the first two leads. If South plays a third trump, West wins the ace, taking dummy's last trump, and forces South in hearts a second time. This leaves West with the only trump in play as well as a fifth heart which will defeat the hand two tricks.

If after two trump leads South switches to the minors, West will ruff the third round of either minor and still defeat the hand one trick. With a club lead, declarer makes four spades without working up a sweat.

In other words, a short-suit lead in a case where you hold four trumps is seldom correct.

5. If you have trump control (A x, A x x, K x, K x x, A Q x, A K x), it's advisable to make a short-suit lead, a singleton or doubleton. Such a lead works murderously well at low-level contracts where partner is apt to have several entries.

If you have a singleton plus trump control and partner has bid or raised your suit, it is universally expected that you will lead the singleton. Then when you get in with your high trump, you can enter partner's hand (hopefully!) by leading his suit or underleading from your own suit. This will enable him to give you a ruff that would have been impossible had you knocked out his entry prematurely. Here's a case in point:

Neither vulnerable
West dealer

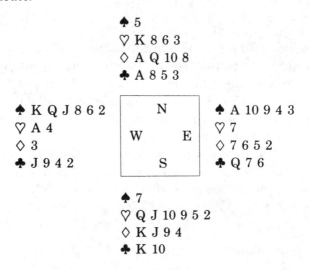

♠ 5
♡ K 8 6 3
◇ A Q 10 8
♣ A 8 5 3

♠ K Q J 8 6 2   ♠ A 10 9 4 3
♡ A 4   ♡ 7
◇ 3   ◇ 7 6 5 2
♣ J 9 4 2   ♣ Q 7 6

♠ 7
♡ Q J 10 9 5 2
◇ K J 9 4
♣ K 10

The bidding:

WEST	NORTH	EAST	SOUTH
1 ♠	Double	4 ♠	5 ♡
All pass			

Sitting West you should lead your diamond in preference to your king of spades. Partner probably has the spade ace, and you want to conserve that entry. You should anticipate getting in with your trump ace and *then* leading a spade to partner's ace for your diamond ruff.

The play might go like this: Declarer wins the diamond in his hand and leads the jack of hearts as if planning to take a finesse in hearts. You've been around too long for a sly trick like that, so you hop up with the ace of hearts and lead a spade. Which spade? Well, although everyone for miles around knows that you led a singleton diamond, partner might not. In order not to give him any problems, lead the queen of spades and *force* him to take his ace. If he doesn't return a diamond for your ruff and the setting trick—well, you've done your best. Next time he invites you to play, tell him you're sick.

6. The lead of a queen or jack from the top of a sequence is easy and comfortable. If you have a trump control, however, and think you can get a ruff somewhere, you're probably better off leading a singleton. Of course, if you are blessed with an ace-king, you have the privilege of making *two* opening leads. First lead the king; and then, when you've seen the board and partner's signal, you should be able to judge what to do next.

7. If you have a hunch and experience has taught you that your hunches are generally good, don't hesitate! But remember: for every unorthodox lead that is written up as a triumph in the newspapers, a thousand are written up *minus* on the score-pads!

Finally, if you are on lead against a slam, consider this advice: Against a small slam when dummy is marked with a long suit, get busy! You must build a trick in a hurry, perhaps by combining a king in your hand with a queen in partner's. You will seldom defeat a small slam by making a passive lead.

If you're defending against a grand slam and your opponents bid it authoritatively, lead passively and let declarer make all the fatal mistakes. After all, he only has to make one! Of course, if they've crept to their contract without using Blackwood, my advice is to lead the suit in which partner has an ace!

He'll be so grateful!

SEVEN

The enemy implies
and you infer

STANLEY: Time passed and I became too occupied with raising a family and attending to what I euphemistically called my "career" to play much bridge. We entertained my father and mother once or twice a month and had noisy sessions in which no single hand was ever played without demonstrated error. My bad game grew steadily worse, whereas my father had become more a perfectionist than ever.

He had discovered duplicate.

In tournament bridge my father had found a perfect arena for his peculiar temperament. Because each hand is conserved to be played over and over again by different pairs of players, he had irrefutable proof that his partners should have bid, played, or defended better. Duplicate bridge is an Elysian field for the results player and will continue to be so until somebody invents a severe penalty for those inspecting a quitted hand with elucidational intent.

Where previously my father had been mildly annoyed at carelessly dropped overtricks, now he raged furiously when his partners failed to milk each hand like it delivered cream. His attention to overtricks extended to rubber bridge, bringing forth such deflationary statements—even in the face of a successful small slam—as, "You should have made an overtrick; in duplicate you'd get a bottom-on-the-board."

More in the interest of curiosity than family unity, I accompanied him to several duplicate sessions. There I discovered that his superior play did not always produce winning results. Although he claimed that duplicate was a far more objective test of a man's ability than rubber bridge—since the luck of the deal was eliminated—he soon learned that tournament bridge had a luck factor that with impish perversity always seemed to go against him.

He suffered miserably when, by an awful stroke of fate, he faced an inexpert player whose empty-headed lead of a singleton king gave him a bottom on the board. It was always his luck when facing a pair of beginners to have flat boards whose results couldn't have been altered by any combination of careless lead or play. Worse, perhaps, was to hear the director call for a skip round just as the newcomers were about to sit down at his table. Passing him by, they went on to deliver gifts like mad Magi on Christmas Eve. Or conversely, it always seemed to be my father's bad luck to be opposed by Lew Mathe when there was a twenty-eight-point slam running opposite, requiring not only inspired mania to bid, but a jettison squeeze to make.

Nevertheless, my father became fairly proficient at duplicate bridge, for he shrewdly acquired the skills that make it one of the most exciting games ever invented. He also, as might have been expected, learned all the customary excuses when he brought in sub-average scores. His zeros came through fixes, whereas his tops were all earned.

He was forced to alter his manners at the game, for groans and slaps at the side of his head, while reluctantly acceptable in our games at home, were highly unethical at duplicate. No longer could he utter an anguished cry of "Oh, no!" following a lead to suggest to the leader that he had made an unwise choice. No longer could he pointedly ask for a review of the bidding while his partner was agonizing over a lead, nor could he aid a puzzled partner in the close-out seat with his repertoire of body twitches, pencil adjustments at the scorepad, or tabling of his cards to imply an opinion that the auction should be terminated.

In the course of my novitiate, he laid down a number of rules, many of which were contrary to my rubber bridge experience.

In rubber bridge, holding

♠ K 10 8 6 5   ♡ 3   ◇ K 5 4   ♣ Q J 4 2

in the south seat after the following auction:

WEST	NORTH	EAST	SOUTH
1 ♡	Pass	Pass	?

he considered any bid unthinkable. He described the action as "opening up a can of worms," for instead of suffering the mere loss of a part-score, we often found West making a forcing bid and East finally coming to life to put them in a makable game.

The first time I passed such a hand in a duplicate session, he fairly flipped. "Bid! Bid! Bid!" he shouted. "You can't let them get off with a cheap part-score! When you're in the balancing seat, balance!"

He instructed me that any bid I might make would presuppose moderate strength in his hand. The presence of a five-card spade suit, he said, was worth a bid with *nothing* in my hand. Fortunately I recognized his hyperbole for what it was, but I think I learned my lesson. His rule of thumb was not bad for those days. Applied to today's point count, it went something like this:

THE ENEMY IMPLIES AND YOU INFER   93

1. Bid with a five-card suit and 8+ points.
2. Double with a shortage of the opening bidder's suit, trump support in the other three, and 10+ points.
3. Bid one notrump with a balanced hand, 12-15 points.

As a corollary to the balancing act, I was also taught to push the opposition to the breaking point in subgame contracts. In rubber bridge it was sheer folly to push the enemy to a part-score of 90 when they might have settled for 30, with 60 above the line. Since in duplicate a part-score bonus of 50 is added to the total score, whether bid or not, there is no disadvantage in forcing the opposition to go to three, for if they make nine tricks in a major suit they score 140 whether they have bid one, two, or three. The advantage of aggressive defensive bidding in duplicate was proved to me time and time again when our opponents were too timid to bid their makable three or doubled us for one-trick sets in our chosen contracts. I can still see the sly smile on my father's face as he wrote down the score on such hands.

"We're compulsive overbidders," he said. "Down one doubled, for minus one hundred," knowing full well that our opponents could have made their three of a minor for +110 or of a major for +140.

Sacrificing was dandy fun at duplicate, for instead of costing money, it often produced tops-on-the-board. It was fatal, however, to go down a doubled trick, or two undoubled tricks, when vulnerable, for no part-score the enemy might amass could top our −200.

Finally, and this was the hardest lesson for me to stomach, I learned to cash out my winning tricks. In rubber bridge my father had taught me that aces were meant to kill kings and queens. He had urged me to grasp at any wild straw to set a contract; but in certain common situations in duplicate, all this was changed.

I was sitting West at a game run by Tom Stoddard at the old Ardmore Club in Los Angeles.

Match points
Both vulnerable
North dealer

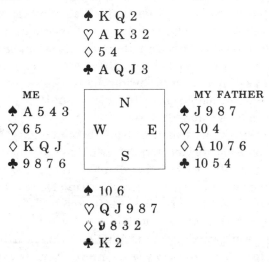

♠ K Q 2
♡ A K 3 2
◇ 5 4
♣ A Q J 3

ME
♠ A 5 4 3
♡ 6 5
◇ K Q J
♣ 9 8 7 6

MY FATHER
♠ J 9 8 7
♡ 10 4
◇ A 10 7 6
♣ 10 5 4

♠ 10 6
♡ Q J 9 8 7
◇ 9 8 3 2
♣ K 2

The bidding:

NORTH	SOUTH
1 ♣	1 ♡
4 ♡	All pass

I led the king of diamonds, and my father gave me an encouraging signal by dropping his seven. I continued with the queen, which also held. Now I paused to think, and my father commenced to squirm. Although he was sincerely opposed to brainlessness in bridge, it caused him acute pain when I showed a necessity to cerebrate. He believed that too much thinking worried the thinker into grave misapprehension. He believed that considerable thought should be expended at the beginning of a hand and a modest reassessment of the count be made whenever an opponent showed a void, but at all other times surplus thinking was as odious as surplus fat. He believed that a game plan should be laid out as soon as the dummy went down and all contingencies expected. He claimed there was a good tactical reason for playing confidently, with brisk certitude: it sapped the confidence of the opponents. He had another reason for playing rapidly. If he deliberated too long over a play, everyone expected him to come up with the right decision. If he played quickly and went wrong, he could always toss it off with a deflating gesture of condescension toward his opponents. "I'm afraid I underestimated you chaps. I should have given that hand a moment's thought."

At any event, my choice of lead on the third trick was the nine of clubs. Declarer let it ride to the king, extracted trumps in two leads, ruffed two diamonds in dummy, and sluffed his two losing spades on his puissant club suit for five-odd. When my father saw my thirteenth card, he screamed like it was a puff adder, not the ace of spades.

"Why didn't you cash out! Six-fifty—that's a bottom on the board for us! I could train a chimp to play his cards better than that!"

"I thought you might have the king of clubs," I said, weakly. He was utterly scornful of my excuse.

"You were looking at the World's Fair in dummy, ten points in your hand and at least four in mine—what in blazes did you think declarer had for his bid?"

I didn't answer him then, for I knew I had goofed. Alas, I make the same mistakes today, for I find it quite difficult to visualize the hidden hand.

KANTAR: You must sharpen up your ability to draw inferences from the bidding and the play. The title of this chapter is somewhat more than an aid to good grammar. It's a strong reminder that everything declarer does or does not do during the course of a hand helps you formulate your game plan. Cards from the hidden hands, partner's and declarer's, add new opportunities for inference. If *you* are declarer, you will be able to draw valid conclusions both from what the opponents do and what they do *not* do. but no matter where you sit, you must keep your antennae waving.

Put yourself in the East seat here, and see how easy it is:

East-West vulnerable
South dealer

DUMMY
♠ 9 7 5
♡ A J 4
◇ J 6
♣ A J 10 9 6

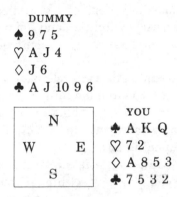

YOU
♠ A K Q
♡ 7 2
◇ A 8 5 3
♣ 7 5 3 2

The bidding:

SOUTH	NORTH
1 ♡	2 ♣
2 ♡	3 ♡
4 ♡	All pass

Your most agreeable partner finds a pleasant opening lead, the three of spades. You win the queen, and declarer plays the four. You know your second spade must live because partner can't have more than five spades and lead the three (Ponder that, my star pupil!) so you play your ace of spades and partner follows with the deuce, showing either two or five spades. It doesn't take a mathematical genius to decide partner has five, because if he has only two, declarer' must have five and that would be inconsistent with the bidding.

Now what to do?

STANLEY: I guess you ought to punch him!

KANTAR: If that means play a third spade, forget it. That would be a waste of time. First of all, you know trumps are breaking well for declarer, and the club suit in dummy is ominous, to say the least. Any honor partner has is finessable, and if he has no club honor, that suit will run easily for diamond discards. Do you have any hope of setting this contract?

STANLEY: I see two possibilities, and I'm not proud of either of them. By some miracle partner might be able to ruff a club——

KANTAR: That wouldn't be a miracle, but it would be unlikely.

STANLEY: You can't blame me for grasping at straws. The other possibility—that partner holds the king of diamonds— seems unlikely, as declarer with an aceless hand has to have *something* for an opening bid.

KANTAR: Good thinking. Put the king of diamonds in declarer's hand and you may *still* set him, if you play your cards right and he plays his wrong. You must hope partner has the queen of diamonds. Shift to a low diamond and put declarer to the guess. Hopefully, he will have noticed your spade honors and playing your partner for the ace of diamonds, he'll duck your diamond to the jack in dummy. If he goes up with the king, get him for your partner next time. But win or lose, you defended properly, remembering that timeless dictum: If it's possible for the enemy to dig his own grave, lend him a shovel. Here's the entire deal:

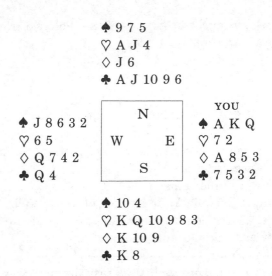

♠ 9 7 5
♡ A J 4
◇ J 6
♣ A J 10 9 6

YOU

♠ J 8 6 3 2   ♠ A K Q
♡ 6 5   ♡ 7 2
◇ Q 7 4 2   ◇ A 8 5 3
♣ Q 4   ♣ 7 5 3 2

♠ 10 4
♡ K Q 10 9 8 3
◇ K 10 9
♣ K 8

STANLEY: I can see where South has a problem. But if he ducks my diamond and partner wins with the queen, I'll die a thousand deaths in the next thirty seconds hoping that he will return the suit so I can take the setting trick.

KANTAR: What partners you must have! Now take this example.

NORTH (DUMMY):   ◇ Q 6

EAST (YOU):   ◇ K 10 7 4

The contract is notrump, and partner leads the three of diamonds. Dummy plays small. What's going on? If declarer had A x or A x x, he would have hoped your partner was leading from the king and would have gone up with the queen to make two tricks in the suit. So he doesn't have the ace but should have the jack. (With x x or x x x he should also play the queen hoping partner has the AK.) Your correct play for first prize is the king, in case declarer has J x.

Similarly, from the other side of the table, no trump again and you lead the three of spades.

DUMMY: ♠ Q 6

WEST (YOU): ♠ J 9 5 3 2

Declarer goes up with the queen, partner the king, and declarer the ace. Who has the ten?

STANLEY: Let me think.

KANTAR: Can't wait. Your partner, of course! If declarer had A 10 x, or A 10 x x, couldn't he assure himself of two tricks by playing low at trick one from dummy?

STANLEY: You make it sound so easy!

KANTAR: It ought to be just as easy for you. Now, let's see how to judge the suit lengths of your opponents. The bidding has gone:

NORTH	SOUTH
1 ♠	2 ♣
2 ♡	2 NT
3 ♣	3 NT
All pass	

What can you infer from this series of bids? You should assume that dummy shows a singleton diamond, since a player who bids two suits and then gives delayed support (not a preference) to a third should have a singleton in the fourth suit. What about the South hand? South heard the bidding, too, yet persists in notrump. Clearly South must have excellent diamonds since he is facing a known singleton. Let's assume you're West and must make an opening lead:

♠ 7 6 3   ♡ J 10   ◇ A 5 4 2   ♣ J 10 6 5

STANLEY: I'd rather lead through strength than up to it, so I must lead one of the majors. But which one?

KANTAR: You're not supposed to answer a question by asking another! You don't make the normal lead of a club, because your partner must be short of clubs. The diamond lead is unattractive because of the lack of intermediate cards. (With something like A J 10 9 you wouldn't worry about leading into strength.) Between the majors, your best shot is hearts, for partner must have at least four and more likely five. How do you know this? By tuning in to the bidding, of course.

You must always assume that if the opponents have an eight-card major suit fit, they'll find it in the bidding. Since North-South don't have eight hearts, they must have seven or fewer. If they have seven, partner must have four, and if they have only six, partner has five! Isn't that simple?

STANLEY: Yes, yes. You've said it before—all I have to do is count!

KANTAR: What else? Now, figure this one out for yourself. You're sitting West holding

♠ A 4   ♡ 10 8 7 5   ◇ 9 7 6 4   ♣ Q J 10

The bidding:

NORTH	SOUTH
1 ◇	2 ♠
2 NT	3 ◇
3 ♠	4 NT
5 ◇	6 ♠
All pass	

What do you lead against this slam?

STANLEY: This is easy! I bet you thought I'd take an hour. I lead a diamond!

KANTAR: Right, but I'm not as surprised as you expected.

Everybody gets one right now and then. Of course you lead a diamond. You would normally lead the queen of clubs, but not on this bidding. They have each bid diamonds, and there's a fine chance that partner has a singleton. With your ace of trumps as a certain entry, your diamond opening looks like money in the bank.

STANLEY: This all sounds so inevitable, like the plot of a TV show. But how can you always trust your opponents' bidding? If they bid like I do, all you'll get from them is murky obfuscation.

KANTAR: Sometimes, but once you've learned to count, you can detect all manner of oily crimes at the bridge table. Take this one:

DUMMY
♠ 10 6
♡ A 8 5
◇ K Q 4 3 2
♣ Q 7 6

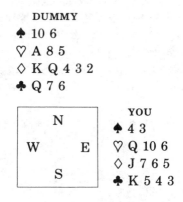

YOU
♠ 4 3
♡ Q 10 6
◇ J 7 6 5
♣ K 5 4 3

The bidding:

SOUTH	WEST	NORTH	EAST
1 NT	Pass	3 NT	All pass

Partner leads the deuce of hearts. That gives you a perfect picture of the heart distribution. Partner should have four and declarer three. But what about the spades? There are nine spades missing between the two hands, and you know partner has four hearts. If he had five spades, he'd undoubtedly have led that suit. Now you can wrinkle your nose and sniff for something rotten in Denmark. You can draw the inference that South, that sneak, has opened one notrump with a five-card spade suit. Furthermore, you know he has three hearts, and the moment the diamond situation reveals itself—diamonds being the suit declarer is most likely to tackle next—you'll have a complete count of the hand.

You can draw inferences not only from the bidding and the play, but from the way your opponents act at the table. Does the opening leader go into a trance before making a lead? Give him something like:

♠ Q J 10 9 3   ♡ A 4 3   ◇ 6 5   ♣ Q 8 7

and the queen of spades will hit the table like it was shot out of a cannon. But let's say he has tranced before leading to this hand, which partner bid to three notrump after your two notrump opening.

♠ 10 9 3
♡ 6 5 3
◇ Q 10 5 4
♣ Q J 3

	N	
W		E
	S	

YOU
♠ A 7 4
♡ A K Q 10
◇ A K 6
♣ 9 8 7

Why doesn't he make a quick lead from the K Q J of spades, or from the ace-king with length in clubs?

STANLEY: Because he doesn't have them. I should say the honors in both suits are split—I pride myself on being able to detect split honors.

KANTAR: You're so clever, Stanley. So he finally leads the deuce of spades and East plays the king. Before you continue any further, how do you assess your chances on this hand?

STANLEY: With guarded pessimism. If the hearts and diamonds break three-three, I can peel nine tricks off the top, but they don't deal hands like that any more, least of all at a bridge lesson!

KANTAR: OK, so you let the king hold, and you hold up again when East continues with the jack. You capture the third spade and start hearts. West follows to the ace, but drops the six of clubs on your king of hearts. Now what?

STANLEY: He has the ace of clubs.

KANTAR: Perhaps, but try to think in terms of distribution!

West has led from a four-card spade suit and has turned up with a singleton heart. That means he has eight cards in the minors. He should have four cards in each, for he probably would have led a five-card suit in preference to a four-card suit headed by the queen. Your play, then, becomes simple. Lay down the ace-king of diamonds, and finesse the ten in dummy. After cashing the queen of diamonds, take the marked heart finesse to fulfill your contract.

STANLEY: I thought this was a lesson on inferences, but you keep talking about *counting*.

KANTAR: You can't separate the two. Here's a hand where they blend together nicely for a perfect finish, but before I show it to you, take note of this clue: As declarer, you must make distributional inferences not only from what the defenders have bid, but from what they have *not* bid.

For example, if one defender has bid a suit and the other has supported it, when you become the declarer and discover that your side has six cards in that suit, you should make the easy assumption that the original bidder had four and his partner three. Also, if they're in the bidding and do not mention a major suit and you later become declarer and see that you have a total of only five cards in that suit, you must assume that their cards are divided 4-4. The reason is obvious: if either opponent held five of the major, he'd surely have mentioned it.

East-West vulnerable
West dealer

DUMMY
♠ K 6 5
♡ 4 3 2
♢ Q 10 5 4
♣ K 9 6

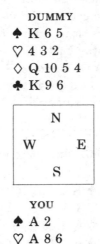

YOU
♠ A 2
♡ A 8 6
♢ 7 6 2
♣ A J 10 8 4

The bidding:

WEST	NORTH	EAST	SOUTH
1 ♢	Pass	1 ♡	2 ♣
2 ♡	3 ♣	All pass	

West opens the king of diamonds, continuing with the ace upon which East discards a spade. When West persists with diamonds, you patiently put in the ten, permitting East to ruff. East now returns a heart. There's no way to avoid losing at least one heart, so the success of your contract depends on how you play trumps. Is there any way you can get a count on the hand at this stage in the proceedings?

STANLEY: With all your ample clues, yes. West started with five diamonds, a fact brought to mind by painful observation. East bid hearts, my side has six, and West supported, so I posit him with three. That leaves five black cards in his hand—bingo! My side has only five spades, so their spades must be divided four-four. West has a singleton club!

KANTAR: Now you're getting the idea—bridge is easy! You go up with the heart ace, lead a club to the king and finesse the jack of clubs on the way back. Show a little class, and don't even look to see what West discards. After all, you *know* this finesse is going to work. Lay down the ace of trumps to snare the queen (I hope you remember that East ruffed once!), and the queen of diamonds on the table will provide a nesting place for one of your losing hearts. You just made your contract—because you counted. Here's the entire hand to prove how well:

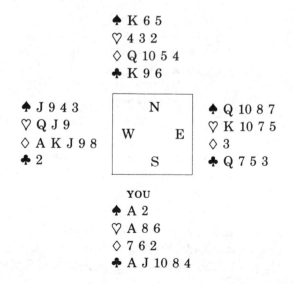

```
              ♠ K 6 5
              ♡ 4 3 2
              ◇ Q 10 5 4
              ♣ K 9 6

  ♠ J 9 4 3        N        ♠ Q 10 8 7
  ♡ Q J 9                   ♡ K 10 7 5
  ◇ A K J 9 8   W     E     ◇ 3
  ♣ 2                       ♣ Q 7 5 3
                   S
              YOU
              ♠ A 2
              ♡ A 8 6
              ◇ 7 6 2
              ♣ A J 10 8 4
```

GAMESMAN BRIDGE

Finally, just to keep you on your toes, let's go back to see if we can catch you on some of the easier inferences:

DUMMY:　♡ 4 3 2

YOU:　♡ J 6 5

West has bid hearts but has led a diamond. What do you infer from his refusal to lead his own suit?

STANLEY: He has the ace-queen and his partner the king. But what do I care if I'm bound to lose all three tricks in this suit?

KANTAR: You might not. Keep West on lead. He was reluctant once, he might still be reluctant. He can't see the king of hearts in dummy, so he might assume you have it. In any event, he'll probably want to get into his partner's hand for a heart lead through your presumed king. In fishing around for East's entry card, West might very well give you a favorable lead.

STANLEY: I wish I could acquire your optimism. When I confront a junky suit like that, I'm inclined to hand in my resignation.

KANTAR: Never do that. Sometimes a hand looks hopeless, but it's amazing how confused defenders can be. Look what happened to me once in a tournament:

Neither vulnerable
South dealer

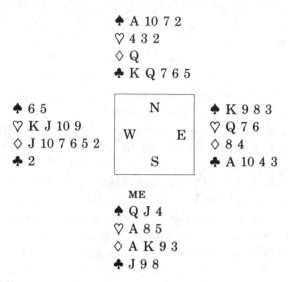

♠ A 10 7 2
♡ 4 3 2
◇ Q
♣ K Q 7 6 5

♠ 6 5
♡ K J 10 9
◇ J 10 7 6 5 2
♣ 2

♠ K 9 8 3
♡ Q 7 6
◇ 8 4
♣ A 10 4 3

ME
♠ Q J 4
♡ A 8 5
◇ A K 9 3
♣ J 9 8

The bidding:

SOUTH	NORTH
1 NT	2 ♣
2 ◇	3 NT
All pass	

The lady opponent playing West led the six of diamonds, which I won with the queen. I promptly led the king of clubs from dummy, just as promptly covered by East with the ace. Now she went into a trance, and by the way she looked about nervously, I knew she had forgotten what her partner had led! Eventually she remembered the color and came out with the six of hearts!

I couldn't afford to duck, because I could count twelve tricks if the spades were 3-3 with the king onside and if the clubs were 3-2, so I went up with the ace of hearts. I then played the queen of spades, and West played the five without

GAMESMAN BRIDGE

hesitation. If I ever saw a lady who would cover an honor with an honor, it was she. I went up with the ace on the table and played a club to my jack. Bad news! West showed out! Now I'd had it. If I were to play with your pessimistic attitude I'd have grabbed my top tricks for down two. But no. I led my jack of spades, captured by East's king, and now, happily enough, she remembered her partner's opening lead! She returned a diamond. I played the ace and king of that suit, nearly falling off my chair when East discarded one of her spades. I took my two good spades in dummy, and East discarded a club! Now my clubs were established, and my opponents ended up taking none of their good hearts. Three notrump bid, making five!

STANLEY: I know. You counted the hand.

KANTAR: I guess so. And I only panicked slightly when things looked hopeless. I just figured I would never tell anybody how few tricks I had taken. Since I took eleven, I'm telling everybody. Now look at this:

DUMMY: ◊ K 4

YOU: ◊ J 10 6

Let's say you opened one notrump, and ended up playing the hand in four spades. West's opening lead was the five of diamonds, and you can afford to lose only one trick in this suit.

STANLEY: I'm fried if I guess wrong.

KANTAR: You might be fried, but you can't possibly guess wrong. Your best play is low from dummy, for it would be a rare player indeed who would underlead an ace, particularly when leading up to the strong hand. I'd lay big odds that the lead was from the queen of diamonds, and the ace lies with East.

STANLEY: Just my luck to have an idiot on lead!

KANTAR: Stop worrying about other people's mentality and listen to this: If North had opened one notrump, a shrewd operator might be underleading an ace through the strong hand, but if you play low a hundred percent of the time you will have the best of the odds by far. Get back to work and watch how you can infer East's spade holding from this sequence: you are declarer at three notrump.

DUMMY

♠ 6 3 2
♡ K Q 7
◇ A 10 9 3 2
♣ K 4

YOU

♠ A 5 4
♡ A 6 5
◇ Q J 5 4
♣ A Q 3

West leads the queen of spades and East plays the seven. You may now presume that East started with K 7 x. But if East overtook the queen with the king, then you should infer that he was unblocking with K x. This could be very important, particularly to duplicate players. If East overtook, you would duck the first trick, assuming K x, and win the spade return. Now if the diamond finesse loses, East will have no more spades and you will make five notrump. If you duck a second round of spades, you will find yourself losing two spades and a diamond, making only four notrump. This is inconsequential to the rubber bridge player but might provide the margin of victory in a tournament.

STANLEY: That's great. So next time I'm in this situation, some sharpie will toss his king away holding K x x and fool me.

KANTAR: When that happens, race right to the phone and tell me his name. He's a man in a million. For years I've been begging my students to play the king from king doubleton when their partner leads the queen. The only time I can be absolutely certain they'll unblock their king is when they have to—it's singleton! And now you're telling me someone is going to pull that play with K x x? Come back to the real world, Jackson!

EIGHT

Placing the cards

STANLEY: My father became ill comparatively young in life, suffering from high blood pressure, coronary occlusions, and all the other normal physical ailments associated with enthusiasm for contract bridge. His doctors warned him that his condition was aggravated by the tensions of the bridge table, but he scoffed at their importunities. The doctors might have had some understanding of the *quantity* of life remaining to him, but they were blindly callous to its quality. My father had no interest in life without bridge. While playing the game, he could forget everything—even his own mortality.

As a dutiful son I sympathized with his philosophy but found myself increasingly unwilling to test its practicality. One of the last times I played with him this explosive hand fell to our lot. As I picked it up, I inquired, "Who dealt?" and my father's oft-repeated answer must serve as a classic in this common situation: "It's always the fool who asks."

North-South vulnerable
South dealer

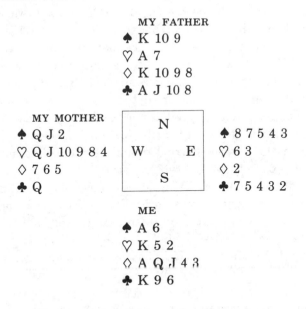

MY FATHER
♠ K 10 9
♡ A 7
◇ K 10 9 8
♣ A J 10 8

MY MOTHER
♠ Q J 2
♡ Q J 10 9 8 4
◇ 7 6 5
♣ Q

N
W   E
S

♠ 8 7 5 4 3
♡ 6 3
◇ 2
♣ 7 5 4 3 2

ME
♠ A 6
♡ K 5 2
◇ A Q J 4 3
♣ K 9 6

Once apprised that I was dealer, I bid a diamond. My mother
made an informative bid of three hearts. The information she
imparted, at least to my father, was that she was busted and
that we probably had a slam. With a baleful glance at his spouse
for her interference, he bid four notrump, showing two aces and
a king of a previously bid suit. I, equally alert to my mother's
obstructionist tactics, bid seven diamonds. Neither her action
nor mine was necessarily conducive to the well-being of a car-
diac, but every bridge player knows how the gentler traits of
character are subverted once you put thirteen cards in hand.
It's like when a man gets behind the wheel of a car.

In any event, I extirpated the trumps and ruffed spades
and hearts, in that order, ending in dummy. I then led the jack
of clubs, losing to the singleton queen, adding one more to my
lifetime collection of monumental swings.

PLACING THE CARDS   113

Although we quickly urged my father to be calm, there was nothing we could do after this hand to mute his explosive roar. His advice, although too late to do me any good, was sound, but based on an instinctual rather than ironclad conviction that my mother could have had no more than one club in her hand. (She had already shown up with six hearts, three diamonds, and at least three spades.) Such careful counting was not in the toolbox of the average player in those days, though now this particular combination provides a textbook exercise for the proper isolation of missing cards. My poor father was almost in tears as he begged me to explain why I hadn't made the insurance play of laying down the ace of clubs.

I realized then that I should no longer play with him. He was living in my guest house in Malibu and we could have had a game every night, but I shuddered at the possibility that I might become an accessory before the fact to his last case of apoplexy. I quit the game cold, playing it rarely during the next fifteen years. (Some of my partners say I resumed much too soon!)

Years later I was to learn I wasn't the only one so affected by playing with my father.

One day he told me that he'd had a good game in a duplicate session the night before with a young assistant coach on the UCLA football team. Years later, when Los Angeles Rams coach Tommy Prothro returned to UCLA after a stretch at Oregon State, I asked him about his bridge game, as I knew he had once considered becoming a pro.

"I haven't played for fifteen years, but I hope to take up tournament bridge again," he said.

"My father played duplicate with a young coach many years ago and I'd always assumed it was you," I said.

"Not likely," said Tommy. "I only played duplicate once."

"Then it must have been some other coach. My father said he was a brilliant player."

"Well, of course, it might have been me," said Tommy,

114   GAMESMAN BRIDGE

slanting toward the action. "I went down to the club in Westwood and they gave me this dignified old gent for a partner. Took the game very seriously. Kept popping nitroglycerin tablets into his mouth."

"That was dad, all right. I had to quit playing with him. I was afraid I might kill him."

Tommy's eyes widened. "Let me tell you about a hand we played near the end of the evening."

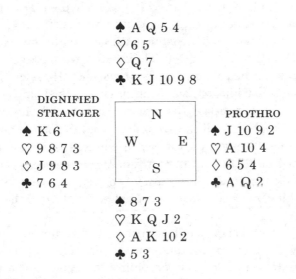

♠ A Q 5 4
♡ 6 5
◇ Q 7
♣ K J 10 9 8

DIGNIFIED
STRANGER
♠ K 6
♡ 9 8 7 3
◇ J 9 8 3
♣ 7 6 4

PROTHRO
♠ J 10 9 2
♡ A 10 4
◇ 6 5 4
♣ A Q 2

♠ 8 7 3
♡ K Q J 2
◇ A K 10 2
♣ 5 3

"North opened a club, South responded a diamond, North bid a spade, and South jumped to three notrump. My partner led the nine of hearts. Declarer took a long time playing to the first trick, and I figured from the way he kept rearranging the cards in his hand that he wasn't counting any higher than eight. So I won the first trick with the ace of hearts and switched to the deuce of spades, right up to the ace-queen in dummy. My partner clutched the edge of the table until his knuckles went white and then hit the nitro bottle again. I hate to think what might have happened to him if it hadn't been the winning play. When declarer went for the clubs, I had another chance to lead spades, setting them up and beating the contract. When the session was over, I figured the game was harder on my nerves than coaching football, so I never went back."

"My father fairly boiled whenever I led up to strength."

"He congratulated me for my brilliance. Said he almost led the king of spades on the opening lead."

"That was my father. He was a magnificent analyst of the *fait accompli*."

At last, of course, it had to happen. He died, exactly as he would have wished, with his boots under a bridge table. He was playing in a championship game with Claire McConnell during Bridge Week in Los Angeles. They had a winning game going for them when he collapsed without warning. He revived briefly as they carried him off, someone having picked up his wallet and put it on his chest. "Don't worry, it's empty," he said, and laughed. What with all the excitement and the strain on Claire, the guy they brought off the bench couldn't hold the lead my father had built up, and they finished only second.

We like to think that wasn't the end, for when St. Peter was looking over my father's résumé, he noticed he played bridge.

We're very fussy about admitting bridge players," he said gloomily. "We set high standards of play and expect angelic decorum at the table. Our seraphim never give gratuitous advice, and we can't abide people who complain about the cards our Beloved Dealer has provided them."

"'Take it the way it comes,' I always said. Make the best of a bad deal, whether in life or bridge."

"I'm glad to hear you say that," said St. Peter, reaching behind his whiskers for a well-worn deck of playing cards. "How do you feel about making a five notrump contract missing an ace, three kings, and two queens?"

"No big thing," said my father. "Give me a favorable lead, a solid eight-card suit, and I can probably bring in all thirteen tricks on a pseudo-squeeze."

"Your distribution is perfectly square," said St. Peter sternly, spreading the cards out on a cloud. The Angel Gabriel sat in dummy's seat and a pair of well-done gentlemen with long pointed tails appeared to play East-West.

"They'll be your escorts to The Other Place in case you don't make this hand," said St. Peter. "Down there you'll spend eternity with partners who count points, lead aces, and always play second hand high."

My father shuddered and looked at the hand. He shuddered again and asked how the bidding had gone.

"It's not important. The bidders were incurable optimists who signed off at five notrump when they realized they were missing an ace. But cheer up. Five notrump ought to be easy, about a fifty percent chance, I should say."

My father had something to say to that but remembered where he was and nodded to the Left Hand Devil to make his opening lead. The five of spades hit the cloud, and my father studied the hand.

♠ 7 6 2
♡ 3 5 6
◊ A Q J 5
♣ 3 2 7

```
        N
    W       E
        S
```

♠ A J 10
♡ A Q J 4
◊ 6 7 8 2
♣ K 5

"Take your time, partner," said the Angel Gabriel, arranging the dummy. "You have about five million years."

My father sighed, thankful at least for the favorable lead. Holding A J 10 in a suit it was a 3 to 1 shot for two tricks, even without the lead. Suddenly he sat up straight in his cloud. The exact percentage for winning two tricks with that combination was 76.2 percent. The Angel Gabriel had put out the spot cards in the dummy in such a way that the seven and six were close together, and the two a little off center.

Gabriel was trying to tell him something!

Quickly my father sought for other clues.

He and the A.G. had seven hearts between them, and Lo! the percentage of a favorable 3-3 split with the opposition was writ all but the decimal point in the dummy's spot hearts—35.6! With eight diamonds in the two hands, he could expect a favorable 3-2 split. Yes, there it was in his hand to the fourth place—67.82 percent!

It was quite unnecessary to look at dummy's club spots. They told him what he already knew, that the percentage in favor of 4-4 with the opposition was 32.7.

What a valuable hand—here were most of the percentages a bridge player really had to know! Of course it didn't seem so valuable for the purpose at hand—making five notrump, but there was nothing else to do but charge ahead, so he did.

The first trick: five of spades, deuce from the dummy, queen from his Right Hand Devil, ace in hand.

My father then led the six of diamonds, not because it was closest to hand, but because he needed all the entries to dummy he could muster. If the diamonds broke, his care in keeping the deuce could be important.

He finessed the diamond successfully and also took the heart finesse. OK, unless that Left Hand Devil was holding up. He led the seven of diamonds, and the king fell from his left. Now back for the second heart finesse. Well, it ought to be obvious, sitting as close as he was to heaven. Both red kings were onside, and both suits broke like angels. On his fourth heart he discarded dummy's deuce of clubs, then he got to dummy with nine tricks in the bag and faced his moment of truth:

DUMMY
♠ 7 6
♣ 7 3

MY FATHER
♠ J 10
♣ K 5

Up to now he'd played the hand as if he'd taken a lesson from you, Eddie. Place all the cards where they have to be to make the contract, and if they aren't there—well, the hell with it.

Along these lines, he realized that if the ace of clubs wasn't with the RHD, he was dead—double-dead, he guessed it should be called. But even that wouldn't do him any good. They'd let him win his king of clubs, and then when he tried to establish his good spade trick, the Left Hand Devil would win with his king and return a club to his partner's ace and small club. Down! Far down. As far as he could go.

It was awful. He stared at the cards over and over again, hoping to find some clue, fearful lest he blow the most fateful play he had ever faced.

He reviewed the play of the cards. The Left Hand Devil had dropped a spade on the thirteenth heart and then two clubs on the last two diamonds. The Right Hand Devil had dropped a club and a—no, it wasn't possible! He also had dropped two clubs!

What dumb defense! No wonder these poor demons had been sent to hell to play bridge through eternity with assorted bid hogs, chronic underbidders, and devils who overtake partner's tricks.

With more hope than confidence, my father led the club seven from dummy. If the Right Hand Devil held the ace of clubs my father didn't care whether he played it or not. The poor devil hesitated before playing his ten, and in that brief moment my father heard a swelling angel chorus. He played his king of clubs, and of course it held, LHD playing the jack. My father than slammed his jack of spades on the cloud, facing his other two cards.

"Claim," he said, "whether you take it or leave it."

Those poor inept devils had discarded to this end position.

They looked at each other sheepishly, swearing they'd do better at their next tournament—The Nether Regional.

My father laughed and clapped St. Peter on the shoulder as he went through the Pearly Gates.

"You were wrong about that being a fifty percent game," he said. "With palookas like that, it was close to a sure thing."

St. Peter winced. He had a feeling those heavenly bridge games would never again be the same.

Here is the entire deal. It's easy to see that RHD needed only to save all his clubs; LHD had to save exactly two spades and two clubs. But then, if they'd played as well as that, my father wouldn't have minded joining them in the Eternal Side Game.

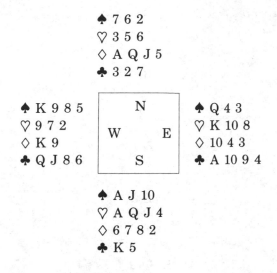

♠ 7 6 2
♡ 3 5 6
♢ A Q J 5
♣ 3 2 7

♠ K 9 8 5   N   ♠ Q 4 3
♡ 9 7 2   ♡ K 10 8
♢ K 9   W   E   ♢ 10 4 3
♣ Q J 8 6   S   ♣ A 10 9 4

♠ A J 10
♡ A Q J 4
♢ 6 7 8 2
♣ K 5

KANTAR: I love that hand. But it only happens like that in heaven. Nevertheless, it's a great demonstration of the principle that you should assume everything works when in hopeless contracts.

Take this for an example. The less said about partner's bidding, the better.

Both vulnerable
South dealer

♠ 7 5
♡ 8 4 3
◇ Q J 10 9 3
♣ K 7 5

ME
♠ A 10 4
♡ K J 10
◇ K 7 5
♣ A Q J 8

The bidding:

SOUTH	NORTH
1 NT	2 NT(!)
3 NT	All pass

West led the three of spades and I let East hold his jack. East continued with the queen, and I ducked again. I finally had to win the third spade (West appeared to have five spades originally) and promptly led the king of diamonds. East won and returned a small heart. What should I do? Remember, my partner's over there biting his nails, *his* judgment being vindicated only if I play right to this trick!

STANLEY: Playing the jack gives West two chances of getting in, while the king gives him only one. So play the king.

KANTAR: Fair enough. Another way of looking at it is that if West has the ace of hearts, you're doomed whatever card you play. Therefore visualize that card with East, and collect your nine tricks by rising casually with the king. This was the deal:

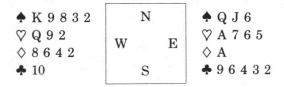

♠ K 9 8 3 2   N   ♠ Q J 6
♡ Q 9 2   W E   ♡ A 7 6 5
◇ 8 6 4 2   ◇ A
♣ 10   S   ♣ 9 6 4 3 2

Incidentally, if East had counted the hand carefully, after he had taken the first two spade tricks, and knowing he had two certain tricks in the red aces, he could have set the contract by switching to a heart.

STANLEY: Very smart. Double dummy.

KANTAR: Not at all. Count the points. East has eleven, and there are only six in dummy. A maximum of eighteen with declarer still gives West two points in addition to the marked king of spades. If these two points are the queen of hearts, the hand is kaput no matter how I might play it.

STANLEY: There's that word again. Count!

KANTAR: Of course. When somebody bids, you count! Even when they don't bid, you count! Here's an example. You have politely kept the bidding open for partner and now find yourself gaping at gaping holes:

♠ A Q J 3
♡ K J
◇ A 9 3 2
♣ 6 5 4

YOU
♠ 10 9 8 7 6
♡ 10 6 3
◇ K Q
♣ 10 8 7

West dealt. The bidding:

WEST	NORTH	EAST	SOUTH
Pass	1 ◇	Pass	1 ♠
Pass	3 ♠	All pass	

West leads the king, queen, and jack of clubs, East signaling high-low and following to the third club. West now puts you to an early test by switching to a small heart. How should you analyze the situation, and what should you do?

STANLEY: I'm three tricks down the drain already, and the ace of hearts is another sure loser for us good guys. If the king of spades is wrong——

KANTAR: Stop! With four certain losers you don't even *think* "if the king of spades is wrong"! You think positive, i.e., "In order to make this hand, the king of spades must lie with West." Now that you've decided this, do some point counting.

STANLEY: Ah! OK. West *must* have the king of spades for three points. He already showed up with six in clubs. With the ace of hearts he'd have had thirteen, enough for an opening bid. Therefore, he doesn't have the ace of hearts. I must play the jack.

KANTAR: Right! You sound as if you know what you are doing. No matter how the cards actually lie, that's the way you must play them! Here's proof:

♠ K 4
♡ Q 8 7 2
◇ 10 8 5 4
♣ K Q J

♠ 5 2
♡ A 9 5 4
◇ J 7 6
♣ A 9 3 2

Here's another hand where you must place your opponents' cards where they will do you the most good.

♠ Q 10 2
♡ 7 6 5 4
◇ A 8 5
♣ J 4 3

YOU
♠ A K
♡ K J 10 9 8
◇ 6 4 3 2
♣ A K

The bidding:

SOUTH	WEST	NORTH	EAST
1 ♡	2 ◇	2 ♡	Pass
4 ♡	All pass		

PLACING THE CARDS

West leads the king of diamonds. How do things look to you?

STANLEY: I have two sure diamond losers and I'm missing the ace-queen-small-small of trumps. So I go up with the ace of diamonds and take the right position in hearts . . .

KANTAR: Which is?

STANLEY: I was hoping you'd tell me.

KANTAR: Concentrate on the queen of hearts for a moment. Let's assume you make a real good guess, playing the jack of hearts to force the ace from West. Do you have any chance of making this contract?

STANLEY: Certainly. He'll take his two winning diamonds and then—ouch!

KANTAR: Double ouch! West will lead a fourth diamond, ruffed in dummy and overruffed by East with the queen. In other words, you can't possibly make this contract if East has the queen of trumps. So you must rise with the king. Success! It holds! You lead another heart and crash the enemy honors. Here are the East-West hands.

```
♠ J 9 8            N          ♠ 7 6 5 4 3
♡ Q 3                         ♡ A 2
♢ K Q J 10 9    W     E       ♢ 7
♣ Q 10 9           S          ♣ 8 7 6 5 2
```

STANLEY: Haven't your opponents ever accused you of peeking?

KANTAR: Sure. There's no greater compliment. Witness this hand, where part-scores of 60 on both sides led to bidding of somewhat less than expert quality.

♠ A 9
♡ 10 9 8 7 6 5
◊ A Q J
♣ 9 2

```
        N
    W       E
        S
```

YOU
♠ J 6 2
♡ Q J
◊ 2
♣ A Q 10 8 6 4 3

The bidding:

WEST	NORTH	EAST	SOUTH
1 ♠	2 ♡ ♪	Pass	3 ♣
Pass	Pass	3 ♠	4 ♣
Pass	Pass	Double	All pass

West led the four of spades, and let's assume you went up with
the ace in dummy, East playing the seven. Without peeking you
ought to be able to place most of the cards. If you listened to
the bidding, that is!

STANLEY: OK. Small spade lead, so the honors are split. The
heart honors are likely to be split, also, so I give West the king
of spades for three points, the ace of hearts for four—and where
are the rest of his points for an opening bid? He must have both
minor suit kings!

KANTAR: There's a way of double-checking your hypothesis
on this hand. What about East? With a part-score of 60, why
didn't East bid directly over two hearts?

STANLEY: One reason is, you warned me the bidding would

be bad. The other, I guess, is that he didn't figure his hand was strong enough for a call. I've given him the queen of spades and the heart king, so he doesn't have either minor suit king.

KANTAR: Pretty good. West's lead and East's pass are strong indicators that the minor suit kings lie with West. Therefore you return to your hand with the club ace, happily felling West's singleton king because you had no other choice, and take the diamond finesse, discarding a major suit loser. Now take the marked club finesse against East's jack, and four clubs doubled comes sailing home.

The East-West hands:

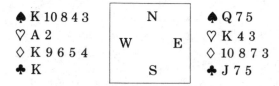

♠ K 10 8 4 3   ♠ Q 7 5
♡ A 2   ♡ K 4 3
◊ K 9 6 5 4   ◊ 10 8 7 3
♣ K   ♣ J 7 5

Now that you recognize the importance of card placing, try this:

♠ K J 7 5
♡ Q 10 4
◊ K Q 6 4
♣ 8 5

YOU
♠ 3 2
♡ A J 8
◊ A J 10 9 7 5
♣ 10 7

The bidding:

NORTH	EAST	SOUTH	WEST
Pass	1 ♣	1 ◊	2 ♣
3 ◊	All pass		

West leads the three of clubs, and East wins the king and ace, West following with the deuce. East turns the guessing over to you by shifting to a trump, discarding a small heart on your second trump play. So there you are: two tricks lost, with the possibility of losing three more. How you play the spades?

STANLEY: Same old problem, king-jack, who's got the ace, who the queen? East opened the bidding, so if you weren't here to twist my arm, I'd take the gloomy view that my king-jack would be swamped.

KANTAR: Why not give yourself the best chance? If you locate the king of hearts *first,* your job in spades might be simplified. Lead the queen of hearts from the table. In this particular hand it happens to be covered by the king. So you know that East started life with the A K J of clubs (West would lead the queen from the queen-jack) and the king of hearts. Certainly West must have at least the ace of spades for his raise. So you lead a spade to the king.

On the other hand, if the heart finesse had *lost* to West's king, you would know that East needed the ace of spades to justify his opening bid. Then you'd finesse your jack.

Here are the East-West hands:

```
      ♠ A 8 6          N          ♠ Q 10 9 4
      ♡ 9 3 2                     ♡ K 7 6 5
      ◊ 3 2        W       E      ◊ 8
      ♣ Q 9 4 3 2      S          ♣ A K J 6
```

Finally, I'd like to show you a hand from a rubber bridge game that showed a high level of card reading.

PLACING THE CARDS   129

♠ A 10 5 4 3
♡ K J
◇ J 9 3
♣ A Q 2

```
        N
    W       E
        S
```

YOU
♠ Q J
♡ Q 10 8 7 5 2
◇ A 10 7 6
♣ 3

The bidding:

WEST	NORTH	EAST	SOUTH
Pass	1 ♠	Pass	2 ♡
Pass	2 NT	Pass	3 ♡
Pass	4 ♡	All pass	

West leads the diamond king, which you win. You lead a low heart to the dummy, and West pops up with the ace. (I expect you'll remember from a previous lesson to unblock your king!) West plays the queen of diamonds and a small diamond which East ruffs. East exits with a small trump which you win with the queen. You've already lost all the tricks you can afford to lose, so which black card finesse do you take? This time I won't object if you take a gloomy view!

STANLEY: Thanks for the clue! Since West held the ace of hearts and the king-queen of diamonds, yet failed to open the bidding, I suspect both black kings are ready to pounce out of the East hand.

KANTAR: That's where they are. So how do you make the contract? You should cash your winning diamond and all your trumps save one, blanking dummy's ace of spades and leaving the clubs in dummy intact. This will be the end position:

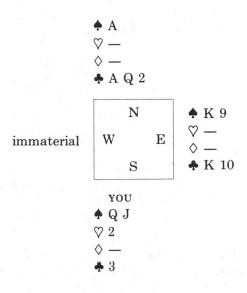

♠ A
♡ —
◊ —
♣ A Q 2

immaterial

N

W   E

S

♠ K 9
♡ —
◊ —
♣ K 10

YOU
♠ Q J
♡ 2
◊ —
♣ 3

You now go to dummy's ace of clubs, trumping out East's king on the next trick. Dummy's ace of spades will provide entry to your good queen of clubs.

Of course if East blanks either black king, you will have to figure out the situation from the discards, or more easily, from East's anguished play.

STANLEY: You're undermining my confidence! I thought if I learned to count I'd eliminate doubt and confusion for-ever!

KANTAR: Hardly that! But if you learn a little more, you'll finally reach that great moment when you can claim you went down on a contract simply because you figured out the hand like an expert.

NINE

Communication

STANLEY: After fifteen years I returned to bridge while living in Rome. An Italian acquaintance took me to the Club di Roma where he assured me I could play in a rubber game with Walter Avarelli and Giorgio Belladonna. I appreciated the honor, but chose to stick to the less exalted company of American tourists and Italians considerably below the rank of world champion.

I won a number of duplicate sessions, and learned to bid in Italian, French, German, and Spanish. I came home to southern California with a highly inflated estimation of my own talent. It wasn't long before I was disabused of this fantasy. I might have been able to communicate in many tongues, but what I communicated had little to do with modern bridge. I'm not talking about new systems of bidding—those will always be with us, and have very little to do with making good bridge players out of bad ones. What astonished me were all the new signals partners used for communication during the play. And the new *lead* conventions—my toes fairly curled when I saw people leading what they called Rusinow—the queen from king-queen!

KANTAR: There you go, throwing the panic switch again. Less than a week from now, you and I are going to play together in a men's pairs regional championship and we'll be up against many new lead conventions, but there is nothing to worry about.

You must never forget that almost every card you lead or play gives some information to your partner. Discipline yourself not to drop cards carelessly while defending a hand. The better your partner, the more inferences he's able to draw from the cards you play. With bad partners, your carelessness might be overlooked, but when playing with a good partner, there's apt to be trouble.

Although many players enjoy using some of the new lead conventions, I think we ought to stick to those you've always played. King from ace-king or king-queen; top of a sequence (jack from jack-ten-nine or jack-ten-eight); and fourth best from a long suit.

Let's begin, not forgetting that these signals are conventions, not rules. They should be used for the communication of information, but should *not* be used where they might cost a trick. Common sense prevails. Many of them you know and use already, but it might be encouraging to see that experts converse in baby talk, too.

1. Against a suit contract you show a doubleton by playing high-low.

DUMMY: ♡ Q 8 6

PARTNER LEADS: ♡ K   YOU: ♡ 10 2

Throw the ten, followed by the deuce, and trump on the third round.

Do not show your doubleton where the loss of your higher card would cost a trick, viz:

DUMMY: ♡ A 10 9

PARTNER LEADS: ♡ K   YOU: ♡ J 2

2. Against a suit contract you also signal high-low to show an honor equal to the one partner has led. You should drop the eight in each of the following circumstances if you want that suit continued:

PARTNER LEADS: ♡ A   YOU HOLD: ♡ K 8 3 2

PARTNER LEADS: ♡ K   YOU HOLD: ♡ Q 8 2

STANLEY: Why distinguish between the two? Both suggest that you want a continuation.

KANTAR: Quite so, but here's where you have to apply your common sense.

DUMMY: ◇ A 3 2

PARTNER LEADS: ◇ K   YOU HOLD: ◇ J 7 4

If declarer plays low from dummy, you should signal with the seven to show an equal honor. But with a doubleton, you would *not* start a high-low, for you wouldn't want a continuation if the cards were distributed like this:

DUMMY: ◇ A 3 2

PARTNER: ◇ K Q 10 8   YOU: ◇ 7 4

DECLARER: ◇ J 9 6 5

3. Against a suit contract you signal high-low to show you can top an unplayed honor in dummy.

DUMMY: ◇ Q 6 3

PARTNER LEADS: ◇ J   YOU HOLD: ◇ K 7 4 or ◇ A 7 4

If dummy plays low to this trick, you signal with the seven.

4. Against a suit contract you signal high-low in trumps if you had three. Here's an example from a tournament where the correct trump signal helped partner to the winning defense. The bidding requires some explanation.

East-West vulnerable
North dealer

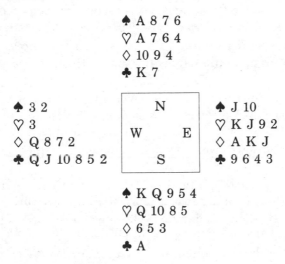

                        ♠ A 8 7 6
                        ♡ A 7 6 4
                        ◊ 10 9 4
                        ♣ K 7

    ♠ 3 2   ♠ J 10
    ♡ 3   ♡ K J 9 2
    ◊ Q 8 7 2   ◊ A K J
    ♣ Q J 10 8 5 2   ♣ 9 6 4 3

                        ♠ K Q 9 5 4
                        ♡ Q 10 8 5
                        ◊ 6 5 3
                        ♣ A

The bidding:

NORTH	EAST	SOUTH	WEST
Pass	Pass *	1 ♠	Pass
2 ♣ **	Pass	2 ◊ ***	Pass
2 ♠ ****	All pass		

*East was a coward not to bid with this hand.

**This is the Drury Convention, a response of two clubs by a passed hand to an opening major suit bid in third seat. It asks partner whether he had a sound opening bid or was opening light.

***The rebid of two diamonds informs partner that the opening was light. (Any other bid would have affirmed a sound opening.)

****Responding hand, properly discouraged, signs off.

The opening lead was the three of hearts, ducked in dummy. East won the king and returned the jack of hearts. (A suit preference signal asking for the return of a diamond, the higher ranking of the remaining non-trump suits, if opening leader could ruff the heart.) West ruffed with the *deuce* of spades and returned the deuce of diamonds to East's king. East returned the nine of hearts, and West ruffed with the three of spades. His return was a low diamond to East's ace. At this point the average player would automatically return his remaining heart for West to ruff. However, West has denied a third trump by ruffing *first* with the deuce and *later* with the three. Had he three trumps he would have ruffed first with the three and then with the deuce!

East decided to trust his partner and, instead of playing a fourth heart, led his jack of diamonds. That was the setting trick. I'm sure you can see that if East had played that heart, South would have won the trick and then discarded his losing diamond on dummy's king of clubs.

5. Signal high-low to show you hold an *even* number of cards in a suit (usually two or four) when declarer leads it first, either from hand or dummy. The obverse of this signal, of course, is that if you hold three or five cards in a suit launched by either declarer or dummy you play your lowest card.

STANLEY: I like this signal, and I beg my partners to play it religiously. But I'm always nervous employing it against an expert declarer. Why give him a clue to the count of the hand?

KANTAR: Stop being nervous! Remember: your first duty is to your partner. He needs help much more than the declarer does. And if he helps you with the count, you'll find new enjoyment of the game and greater understanding. When you become a bona fide expert you can fool partner, but only if he believes you when you tell him you're an expert.

Notice how important it is for partner to give you a count in this suit.

DUMMY: ♡ A K 3

YOU: ♡ J 9 7 2   PARTNER: ♡ 6 5 4

DECLARER: ♡ Q 10 8

Declarer goes to dummy with the ace of hearts, and partner plays his four, the same card he'd play if he were a raw beginner. But he *isn't* a beginner, and you can figure him for three cards exactly. Let's now assume that declarer's only hope of making his contract is to execute a pseudo squeeze. He runs off a long side suit, and you are forced to make discards. Since you know declarer can't have four hearts, you can discard yours with careless abandon.

The greatest advantage you can derive from this signal is when you are defending against a contract where a long side suit lies in an otherwise entryless dummy.

DUMMY: ♡ K Q J 10 9

YOU: ♡ A 5 4   PARTNER: ♡ 8 7 6

DECLARER: ♡ 3 2

Declarer leads his deuce to the king in dummy, partner dropping the six. When partner follows with his seven to dummy's queen, you know the distribution is as shown, and you collect your ace, leaving those established cards dead in dummy. With only two cards in hand, partner of course would have signaled high-low to enable you to wait till the third round to win with your ace.

6. When partner leads low in a suit and your high card in the third seat holds the trick, return your *original* fourth best card if you started with four or more in the suit. With three cards simply return your higher remaining card.

COMMUNICATION   137

PARTNER LEADS: ♡ 4   YOU HOLD: (a) ♡ A 5 3 2
                                        (b) ♡ A 5 2
                                        (c) ♡ A 2

In all three cases you win with the ace, then return (a) the deuce, (b) the five, and (c) the deuce.

STANLEY: How will partner know the difference between the first and third cases?

KANTAR: Sometimes he won't, but a good partner can usually tell whether you have two or four in the suit. What helps him most is when you return your smallest card—he knows you didn't start life with *three* cards in the suit!

7. When partner leads an ace against a notrump contract he normally guarantees a strong suit such as A K Q 10 . . . , A Q J 10 . . . ,* A K J 10 . . . , A K J 3 2 . . . , or even A K 10 9 2, and he expects you to (a) drop your high honor (king, queen, or jack) under the ace or (b) lacking such a card, give him a distributional count. If you have a doubleton, play high. With three, play low. With four, play second highest. Some bridge books instruct you to throw your highest card, whether it's an honor or not. These books are outdated. See how this modern system works.

DUMMY: ♠ 7 6

ME: ♠ A K Q 10 2   YOU: ♠ 9 4

DECLARER: ♠ J 8 5 3

---

*Lacking an outside entry, you should lead the queen from A Q J 10 . . . The use of three dots in this and other examples suggests a suit of indeterminate length—four, five, or ? cards.

I lead the ace, you drop the nine. You have now told me two things. You don't have the jack and you have no more than two cards in the suit. I will then shift and wait for you to lead through declarer's guarded jack.

STANLEY: What if the nine were a singleton?

KANTAR: Unlikely, because declarer would probably have bid the suit holding five cards. Change one card in the suit and you have:

DUMMY: ♠ 7 6

ME: ♠ A K Q 10 2   YOU: ♠ 9 4 3

DECLARER: ♠ J 8 5

Now after I've led the ace, you drop your three and I know I can pick up the jack and run the suit. This is obviously a marked improvement over the old system where automatically dropping the nine would tell me nothing except that you didn't have the jack.

8. When partner leads a king against a notrump contract, signal when you have a high honor (ace, queen, or jack) by dropping your next highest card. Lacking any of those honors, play your smallest card.

STANLEY: What if the honors are doubleton?

KANTAR: Easy. A person leading a king against a notrump contract generally holds K Q J or K Q 10. Therefore, if you have a doubleton headed by an honor you proceed as follows: A x, overtake with the ace and return the small card. Q x, play small, as partner doubtless cannot afford to have you jettison your queen, or he'd have led his ace in the first place. J x, unblock the jack if dummy has two or three small cards in the suit. If dummy holds 10 x x or 9 x x x, you'd better preserve the jack.

9. When partner leads a queen against notrump, signal high-low to indicate the possession of the ace, king, or ten, otherwise, play low to deny the honor. With a doubleton ten the unblock is usually right, depending upon dummy.

10. Against trump or notrump contracts the lead of a jack denies a higher honor. Put yourself in this situation, and try to tell me what you think declarer holds:

DUMMY: ♡ 7 6 4

PARTNER LEADS: ♡ J   YOU HOLD: ♡ A 5 2

DECLARER: ♡ ?

If partner is leading from K J 10, you ought to take the Ace and return the suit quickly to rattle off the first four or five tricks. But what if the jack is partner's top card? A switch of suit might well be in order, for declarer's king and queen will certainly put a crimp in your momentum.

See how comfortably it works on this hand. South deals.

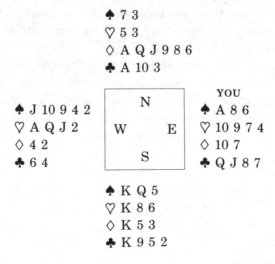

♠ 7 3
♡ 5 3
◇ A Q J 9 8 6
♣ A 10 3

♠ J 10 9 4 2   YOU
♡ A Q J 2   ♠ A 8 6
◇ 4 2   ♡ 10 9 7 4
♣ 6 4   ◇ 10 7
          ♣ Q J 8 7

♠ K Q 5
♡ K 8 6
◇ K 5 3
♣ K 9 5 2

The bidding:

SOUTH	NORTH
1 ♣	1 ◇
1 NT	3 NT
All pass	

Partner has led the jack of spades, and, using traditional methods, you haven't any idea what to do next. If he has led from K J 10 plus, you'd better stick to spades. But nowadays you know exactly what to do. Your partner has nothing above the jack, so win the ace and shift to hearts before the diamond onslaught begins.

STANLEY: Very good, Eddie. But what about—

KANTAR: I know, I know. What do you lead when you have the A J 10 or K J 10? Answer: The ten!

STANLEY: Ouch! The lower of touching honors? Are you some kind of radical or something?

KANTAR: Not at all. I'm the bearer of good tidings. This is a lead convention that works.

11. Against suit or notrump contracts, the lead of a 10 or 9 either denies a higher honor or *guarantees* two higher, one being the next touching. When partner leads a ten, it is either top of a sequence, a doubleton, a singleton, or from A J 10 or K J 10. If you can see the jack, you *know* that partner has no higher honor. The same holds for the lead of the nine— sequence, doubleton, singleton, or A 10 9, K 10 9, or Q 10 9 without exception.** (Also lead the nine from A K 10 9 or A Q 10 9 combinations.) Furthermore, if you can see the ten you know partner's nine is his highest card.

12. When partner leads a small card vs. a notrump contract and dummy wins the trick with the ace or king, give a high-card signal if you hold the king or queen.

** Against *notrump* contracts the lead of a nine will almost invariably show two higher honors, as top of nothing is rarely led in expert circles. Against *trump* contracts, however, the lead of a nine may well indicate a doubleton or singleton.

DUMMY: ♠ A 7

PARTNER: ♠ J 10 4 3 2   YOU: ♠ Q 9 6

DECLARER: ♠ K 8 5

Partner leads the three of spades. If dummy plays the ace, you must play the nine to indicate either the king or queen.

13. Against notrump contracts, when partner leads small and dummy wins the trick with the *queen* or lower, give ~~your~~ partner a distributional signal—high with a doubleton, low from three, and second high from four—just as if partner had led the ace and you didn't have an honor to throw.

Notice how brilliantly you'd be able to defend this hand if partner gave you a distributional count:

DUMMY
♠ J 10 9
♡ J 10 9
◇ K 8 4
♣ A 10 8 4

YOU   PARTNER
♠ A Q 8 4 3   N   ♠ 7 5
♡ K 7 6   W   E   ♡ 8 5 4
◇ 10 9 3   ◇ J 7 6 5
♣ 9 6   S   ♣ K 7 5 2

♠ K 6 2
♡ A Q 3 2
◇ A Q 2
♣ Q J 3

The bidding:

SOUTH	WEST	NORTH	EAST
1 NT	Pass	3 NT	All pass

You lead the four of spades, and dummy's nine holds the trick. Partner, unable to beat the card in dummy, gives you a count signal with the seven. You know he has a doubleton, so when declarer finesses the jack of hearts and you take the king, you do not continue spades. You know declarer's king is guarded. You get out with the ten of diamonds, and there is no way declarer can count nine safe tricks. He takes the club finesse, and when this loses the spade return is devastating.

The previous hand may look easy to defend, but let's change it slightly.

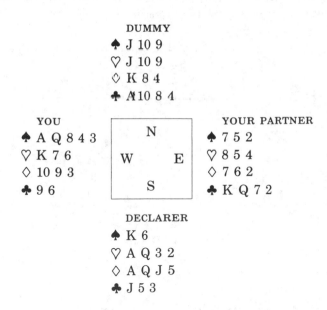

DUMMY
♠ J 10 9
♡ J 10 9
◇ K 8 4
♣ A 10 8 4

YOU
♠ A Q 8 4 3
♡ K 7 6
◇ 10 9 3
♣ 9 6

YOUR PARTNER
♠ 7 5 2
♡ 8 5 4
◇ 7 6 2
♣ K Q 7 2

DECLARER
♠ K 6
♡ A Q 3 2
◇ A Q J 5
♣ J 5 3

The bidding is exactly the same, and you and dummy have identical hands. Partner is a point stronger, but unless you play this one exactly right, declarer can bring in nine tricks easily.

You lead the four of spades again, but this time partner drops the deuce. You know he's not being careless, just throwing his lowest card; you know his card is a *signal,* showing three. So, when the heart finesse is made your way, you can murmur a somewhat unethical "Down one!" to the declarer as you cash your ace of spades, catching his king.

STANLEY: I play in a game where you don't murmur that stuff—you spread your four spades on the table and shout, "Start discarding!"

KANTAR: Then maybe these lessons will improve your manners, if not your game!

14. When defending against a trump contract, and leading a suit you know partner can ruff, give him a suit preference signal to indicate the suit you wish him to return. Here is the suit preference signal in its classic form.

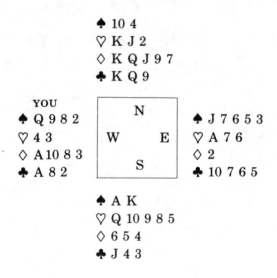

```
                    ♠ 10 4
                    ♡ K J 2
                    ◇ K Q J 9 7
                    ♣ K Q 9

    YOU                 N
    ♠ Q 9 8 2                       ♠ J 7 6 5 3
    ♡ 4 3           W       E       ♡ A 7 6
    ◇ A 10 8 3                      ◇ 2
    ♣ A 8 2             S           ♣ 10 7 6 5

                    ♠ A K
                    ♡ Q 10 9 8 5
                    ◇ 6 5 4
                    ♣ J 4 3
```

Bidding, vulnerability, and all that are immaterial. South is in a four-heart contract and you have opened the deuce of spades, won by declarer with the ace. He promptly goes after trumps, whereupon your partner takes his ace and instead of returning your spade lead, plays the deuce of diamonds. In the face of that dummy, even you recognize it as a singleton, so you win with the ace and return a diamond for partner to trump. But which diamond?

STANLEY: The answer is easy, since I know the subject of the lesson. Since I want a club return in order to give partner a second ruff, I use the suit preference signal, leading a low diamond to indicate the *lower* of the two remaining suits.

KANTAR: Good. And conversely, if instead of the ace of clubs you held the king of spades—

STANLEY: I'd have returned the eighteen of diamonds.

KANTAR: I don't care what you call it as long as it's high enough to indicate you want the higher ranking suit returned.

15. A suit preference signal may be made in response to an opening lead when the appearance of dummy suggests that the signal *cannot possibly* refer to a continuation of the suit.

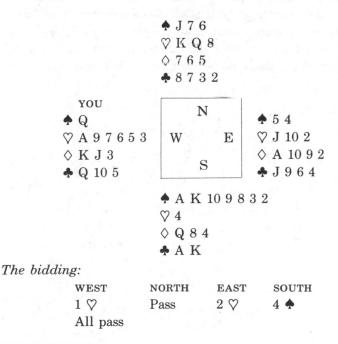

```
                    ♠ J 7 6
                    ♡ K Q 8
                    ◊ 7 6 5
                    ♣ 8 7 3 2

      YOU                N           ♠ 5 4
   ♠ Q                               ♡ J 10 2
   ♡ A 9 7 6 5 3    W       E        ◊ A 10 9 2
   ◊ K J 3                           ♣ J 9 6 4
   ♣ Q 10 5             S

                    ♠ A K 10 9 8 3 2
                    ♡ 4
                    ◊ Q 8 4
                    ♣ A K
```

The bidding:

WEST	NORTH	EAST	SOUTH
1 ♡	Pass	2 ♡	4 ♠
All pass			

You have led the ace of hearts, and it's absolutely impossible for partner to want a continuation. He has given you a raise, so he has at least three. (*Only* three, you hope!) Therefore, this is a golden opportunity for him to help you make your inevitable switch. He will play a high card to imply diamonds or a low card to call for clubs. The jack of hearts is a clear call for diamonds. You lead small; he'll take his ace and return the suit, setting the contract.

But please remember, this signal is given only when the appearance of the dummy *and* the bidding on the hand make it obvious that a shift *must* be made. Thus if partner had not supported hearts, it would be dangerous to play the jack, for fear you might read it as singleton or doubleton. It would be wiser for him to play low with three and hope you guess the right shift.

You must be extremely wary of this signal when the dummy has a singleton and partner gives you an encouraging signal. Is he suggesting a continuation or is he giving a suit preference signal asking for the higher ranking of the two remaining side suits? How would you read partner's signal in this hand? (North deals.)

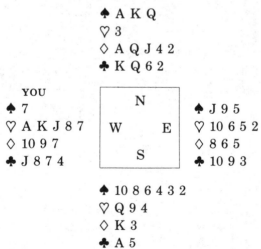

$$\spadesuit \text{ A K Q}$$
$$\heartsuit \text{ 3}$$
$$\diamondsuit \text{ A Q J 4 2}$$
$$\clubsuit \text{ K Q 6 2}$$

YOU
$$\spadesuit \text{ 7}$$
$$\heartsuit \text{ A K J 8 7}$$
$$\diamondsuit \text{ 10 9 7}$$
$$\clubsuit \text{ J 8 7 4}$$

$$\spadesuit \text{ J 9 5}$$
$$\heartsuit \text{ 10 6 5 2}$$
$$\diamondsuit \text{ 8 6 5}$$
$$\clubsuit \text{ 10 9 3}$$

$$\spadesuit \text{ 10 8 6 4 3 2}$$
$$\heartsuit \text{ Q 9 4}$$
$$\diamondsuit \text{ K 3}$$
$$\clubsuit \text{ A 5}$$

The bidding:

NORTH	SOUTH
1 ◇	1 ♠
3 ♣	3 ♠
4 NT	5 ◇
6 ♠	All pass

You lead the king of hearts, and partner plays the ten.* Is he calling for a continuation, or is it a suit preference signal requesting a diamond shift?

STANLEY: I remember that hand, or one of its lineal ancestors! My partner gave me the ten of hearts. Since I had just learned this new signal, I obediently switched to a diamond. Oh, was he sad!

KANTAR: I should think so, because his come-on was exactly that. He knew the heart continuation would sink the slam. You play the ace of hearts, and when dummy trumps, partner's jack of spades becomes the setting trick.

Remember, a high signal from partner is not a suit preference signal if there's the slightest chance for trump promotion. In other words, when dummy has a singleton, be alert to the possibility that partner may want to promote a trump trick for himself.

16. Finally, we come to the most common and most important signal of them all—the Common Sense Signal—high card to suggest a continuation, low card to suggest a switch.

STANLEY: Back to basics. When I first learned the game, that's the only signal there was!

---

*In an expert partnership, the six should be sufficient to insure a continuation—reserving honor plays for suit preference purposes—except the king under the ace which shows solidity, or the queen under the king which promises the jack.

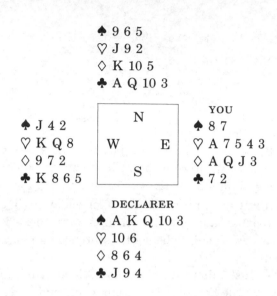

♠ 9 6 5
♡ J 9 2
◇ K 10 5
♣ A Q 10 3

YOU
♠ 8 7
♡ A 7 5 4 3
◇ A Q J 3
♣ 7 2

♠ J 4 2
♡ K Q 8
◇ 9 7 2
♣ K 8 6 5

N
W   E
S

DECLARER
♠ A K Q 10 3
♡ 10 6
◇ 8 6 4
♣ J 9 4

The bidding:

NORTH	EAST	SOUTH	WEST
Pass	1 ♡	1 ♠	2 ♡
2 ♠	All pass		

Your partner, West, has led the king of hearts, and you have an equal honor, the ace. Although you would usually play high to signal partner that you have an equal honor, the reason for playing high would *not be to show the equal honor as much as to recommend a continuation of hearts.* If for any reason partner of the opening leader wishes a switch to a different suit, he should play low.

On this hand, obviously, you want a diamond switch, and you hope partner will be able to figure this out by looking at his own hand and the dummy. If he doesn't have the king of clubs, he might guess wrong, but at least you must give him the chance to guess right! With the help of your signal (the heart three) he will lead a diamond, you'll return a small heart to his queen, and he'll lead another diamond. Your play of the thirteenth diamond will establish partner's jack of trumps for the setting trick.

An even more spectacular example of using common sense in signaling is shown in the following:

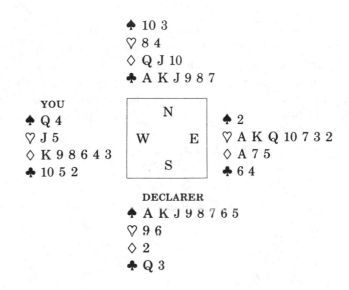

♠ 10 3
♡ 8 4
◇ Q J 10
♣ A K J 9 8 7

YOU
♠ Q 4
♡ J 5
◇ K 9 8 6 4 3
♣ 10 5 2

♠ 2
♡ A K Q 10 7 3 2
◇ A 7 5
♣ 6 4

DECLARER
♠ A K J 9 8 7 6 5
♡ 9 6
◇ 2
♣ Q 3

The bidding:

NORTH	EAST	SOUTH	WEST
1 ♣	4 ♡	4 ♠	All pass

By the time the bidding gets around to you it is too high for safe action. You lead your jack of hearts, and partner overtakes to cash a second round of hearts. At trick three partner plays the ace of diamonds. Which diamond do you play, and why?

STANLEY: I have an equal honor in diamonds, but I'm much more interested in ruffing a heart with my queen of spades, the guaranteed setting trick. I can't be absolutely certain my partner will understand, but I must give him a *chance* by discouraging him with the three of diamonds.

KANTAR: Right! If you didn't have a high spade, you'd have encouraged him to continue diamonds.

The whole trick to the Common Sense Signal is simply to ask yourself one question: Do I want the suit that my partner has led continued? If the answer is yes, play a big card. If no, play a small one.

Now that you and partner understand each other, you will assume that a low card played under the lead of an ace or king usually indicates possession of strength in another suit. Therefore you must occasionally give false encouragement in the suit led in order to prevent partner from making a disastrous shift. Here the Common Sense Signal reaches its apogee:

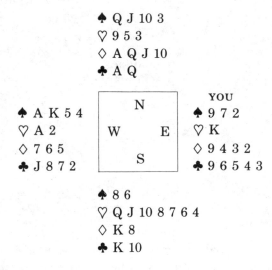

♠ Q J 10 3
♡ 9 5 3
◇ A Q J 10
♣ A Q

♠ A K 5 4　　　　　　YOU
♡ A 2　　　　　　　♠ 9 7 2
◇ 7 6 5　　　　　　♡ K
♣ J 8 7 2　　　　　◇ 9 4 3 2
　　　　　　　　　　♣ 9 6 5 4 3

♠ 8 6
♡ Q J 10 8 7 6 4
◇ K 8
♣ K 10

The bidding:

NORTH	EAST	SOUTH	WEST
1 NT	Pass	4 ♡	All pass

Your partner has led the king of spades. If you were to play from habit, without thinking, you would drop the deuce of spades. With that dummy staring him in the face, your partner would quite logically expect you were asking for an immediate shift. Whichever minor suit he switches to will give the game to the opposition—since declarer will discard a spade on the third diamond before drawing trumps. Therefore, your common sense should impel you to start a false signal by dropping the seven of spades. Partner will continue with the ace of spades, and later you'll win two trump tricks. Since you lack both minor suit kings, you *know* declarer will be able to dispose of any spade loser he may have on the diamonds.

STANLEY: What you said earlier is true—there's no such thing as a meaningless discard. But it's often difficult to get your meaning across with a single card.

KANTAR: And how well I know it! I once had a pupil who experienced considerable difficulty with discards, so I gave her a number of cautionary rules to follow.

1. Seldom void yourself in a suit, as this will make it easy for declarer to finesse partner's honors.

2. Keep length parity with dummy, to prevent declarer from setting up dummy's suit.

3. Try to avoid discarding cards in a suit declarer has bid, lest you make it easier for him to set it up.

4. Avoid sluffing high cards such as nines and tens in short suits, as they frequently take tricks.

5. In general, discard from long suits you don't want partner to lead, saving good cards in the suit or suits you do want him to lead.

Good advice, to be sure, but look what happened when my pupil picked up the West hand in the following deal.

Neither vulnerable
North dealer

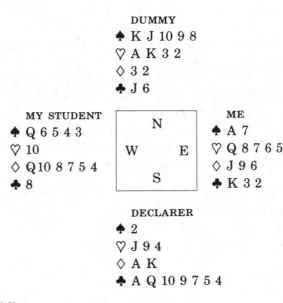

DUMMY
♠ K J 10 9 8
♡ A K 3 2
◇ 3 2
♣ J 6

MY STUDENT
♠ Q 6 5 4 3
♡ 10
◇ Q10 8 7 5 4
♣ 8

ME
♠ A 7
♡ Q 8 7 6 5
◇ J 9 6
♣ K 3 2

DECLARER
♠ 2
♡ J 9 4
◇ A K
♣ A Q 10 9 7 5 4

The bidding:

NORTH	SOUTH
1 ♠	2 ♣
2 ♡	3 ◇
3 ♠	3 NT
All pass	

Faced with leading a suit bid by the opponents, she chose the ten of hearts, ducked in dummy. I won the queen and, because I was eager to knock out the entry to dummy's spades, returned a second round of hearts. South won the jack, and my partner had to make a discard. Although it might seem routine to discard a small spade, that's only if you don't have rules to remember.

I had told her about keeping length parity with the dummy, so she decided she couldn't discard a spade. Of course that rule is constantly broken when one's spots aren't good enough, but a rule's a rule, so my partner turned her attention to the diamond suit.

Well, there was that rule about not discarding from a suit that declarer has bid. Of course, that applies to holding on to four cards of declarer's second suit in order to prevent the suit from being run later. With this hand it wouldn't be too terrible to discard a diamond, although a spade is better. But a rule is still a rule, so she had to dip down to the club suit.

She had only one club. Discarding it would violate the rule about voiding yourself prematurely in a suit lest declarer finesse your partner out of his eyeballs.

So what to do? She finally cracked and made the worst possible choice—the eight of clubs. But in the end, her inferior selection produced a superior result. Declarer thought her discard showed the king of clubs and refused the finesse! We achieved an excellent match point result on the hand, despite the shrewd analysis of it made by a kibitzer: "You squeezed your partner—with too many rules, that is."

STANLEY: You don't have to worry about my getting all tangled up in rules. I'm a dues-paying icon smasher!

KANTAR: I *do* have to worry, for next week you'll be my partner. Why do you think I've worked so hard to get you to communicate?

STANLEY: Because you're a dreamer. You hope these seeds you've planted will become beautiful roses.

KANTAR: I'll be satisfied if I get dandelions.

TEN

Conflict!

STANLEY: My mentor, who has played in international competition with and against the best players in the world, occasionally partners his students in big tournaments. He finally said I was ready for the Men's Pairs event at Los Angeles's prestigious Bridge Week, the largest of the more than seventy-five annual regionals in the United States.

We found ourselves in competition with 179 other pairs, separated into six sections of fifteen tables each. The competition was stiff, but I realized from the outset that my chief adversary was myself. As I found my seat in the South position, Table 1 in Section C, and looked across at partner I realized I had reached a point of utter absurdity. Having Eddie Kantar turn dummy's cards to my fumbling declarer play would be like inviting Van Cliburn in to hear me play "Sentimental Journey" on the piano. Even Arnold Palmer couldn't win a tournament if his caddie lied to him about the length of the holes, kicked his approach shots into the rough, and grabbed the putter out of his hands whenever the green was hard to read.

I had heard that most players choke up when they come to the table of an expert. If so, the match was about even, for whatever advantage Eddie enjoyed in facing choked-up opponents was offset by the fact that he was playing with a choked-up partner!

We had discussed the conventions we intended to use some days in advance, and Eddie's advice on the subject was sound. The newer the partnership, the fewer the conventions.

We would play strong notrumps (16-18), weak two-bids (6-12), and preemptive jump overcalls. We would open four-card major suits, and bid Landy and Michaels in competition. I selected these because they are similar and simple, showing interest in the major suits and a compulsion to compete.

In the interest of conserving space, we're including here only the most dramatic or instructive of the fifty-two boards we played. The two sessions are designated by Roman numerals, with the cardinal numbers being those of the boards. I was played on a Tuesday afternoon, and II the afternoon following. Eddie was North and I was South in the first session; he was East and I was West in the second.

Neither vulnerable
South dealer (I, 11)

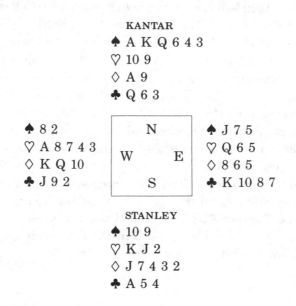

KANTAR
♠ A K Q 6 4 3
♡ 10 9
◇ A 9
♣ Q 6 3

♠ 8 2
♡ A 8 7 4 3
◇ K Q 10
♣ J 9 2

♠ J 7 5
♡ Q 6 5
◇ 8 6 5
♣ K 10 8 7

STANLEY
♠ 10 9
♡ K J 2
◇ J 7 4 3 2
♣ A 5 4

The bidding:

SOUTH	NORTH
Pass	1 ♠
1 NT	2 NT!
3 NT	All pass

STANLEY: I consider Eddie's bid of two notrump a master bid, as well as an evidence of generosity rarely seen among bridge players.

KANTAR: Generosity had nothing to do with it. My bid was based on pure greed. A hand like mine will usually play better at notrump. Even if you lacked the values to go to game, you might make three for +150, scoring better than those in three spades, which is all it figures to make. After all, the odds are good that I have seven tricks for you.

STANLEY: Six! I blew the hand right out of the sky! The opening lead was the four of hearts, covered by nine, queen, and king. I led a heart, taken by West with his ace, and he put me on the board with a spade! Now any fool could run ten tricks, but not me! I ran the spades, came to my hand with the ace of clubs, and cashed the king of hearts. West had dropped the jack of clubs on the ace and had no more hearts, so I got brilliant. On my king of hearts I bared my ace of diamonds in dummy, leaving this end position:

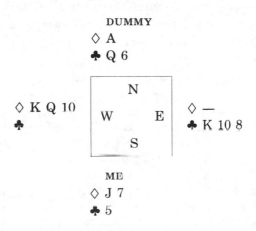

DUMMY
◊ A
♣ Q 6

◊ K Q 10
♣

◊ —
♣ K 10 8

ME
◊ J 7
♣ 5

I led the five of clubs, expecting West to play his king, making the dummy good for a brilliant five notrump.

West showed out, and East took the king, ten, and eight of clubs for a gloomy three notrump. You will notice that I never did cash my ace of diamonds.

KANTAR: I noticed. I was a witness to the whole affair. There's very little a teacher can say about the play of a hand like this. At rubber bridge, your play would have gone unnoticed, but at duplicate it was silly. You should have analyzed the hand from the start, deciding that few pairs would be playing the hand at notrump. Four notrump, earning you +430 would be an excellent score, but absolutely essential to make in case anyone was able to bid and make four spades for +420. As it turned out, we were lucky, for only one pair made that score in our section. But in other sections, many players bid and made four spades, and twenty-five out of seventy-eight pairs shared my "brilliance" by playing the contract at notrump.

STANLEY: It becomes more and more obvious that I have a lot to learn. And to show the reader who might not play duplicate how important it is to win overtricks, I have broken down the results of this board in our section. Thirteen pairs play each board, and a pair wins 1 match point for every other pair they beat, and ½ match point for each tie. The same board was also played in the other five sections, but the results there did not affect our score.

Contract and result	Score	North-South match points	East-West match points
3 NT, making 5 (two pairs)	+460*	11½	½
3 NT, making 4	+430	10	2
4 ♠, making 4	+420	9	3
3 NT, making 3 (us!)	+400	8 [9½]***	4
3 ♠, making 5	+200**	7	5
3 ♠, making 4 (six pairs)	+170	3½	8½****
3 ♠, making 3	+140	0	12

*Trick score 100, extra tricks 60, game bonus (not vulnerable) 300.

**Trick score 90, extra tricks 60, part-score bonus 50.

***The bracketed figure represents the match points we would have earned if I had made four notrump, tying with one other team and therefore sharing 10 and 9 match points.

****East-West pairs played a passive role in the bidding of this board, but note their rewarding match point score if their opponents failed to bid game and were held to ten tricks!

North-South vulnerable
South dealer (I, 15)

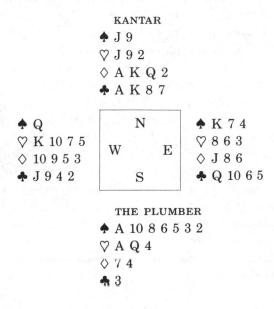

KANTAR
♠ J 9
♡ J 9 2
◇ A K Q 2
♣ A K 8 7

♠ Q
♡ K 10 7 5
◇ 10 9 5 3
♣ J 9 4 2

♠ K 7 4
♡ 8 6 3
◇ J 8 6
♣ Q 10 6 5

THE PLUMBER
♠ A 10 8 6 5 3 2
♡ A Q 4
◇ 7 4
♣ 3

The bidding:

SOUTH	NORTH
1 ♠	3 NT
4 ♠ ????	All pass

STANLEY: Not putting this contract in six spades, after being guaranteed sixteen high-card points by partner, or at least exploring the slam by bidding Blackwood is the act of a craven coward. We earned only 5½ match points on this hand, where we should have earned 10½ by bidding the ice-cold slam.

KANTAR: Not really. First of all, my response of three no-trump left a little to be desired, and since you were going to play the hand the way you did, I figure your bid *saved* us 2 match points.

STANLEY: That's not fair! As soon as the hand went down,

I realized I had blown the bid, so I got flustered and blew the play. If I'd been in a slam I might have remembered your lessons. I won the opening lead of a small diamond on the board and took a losing spade finesse. Next time I got to the board, I led a spade again and played for the drop!

KANTAR: Ye gods, you've become a master of ineptitude! If you were going to play for the drop, why didn't you put down your ace in the first place? By taking the finesse and *then* playing for the drop you were betting on the 6+ percent chance of a stiff king-queen to your left, a mathematically absurd way of playing. It isn't as though I've loaded you with a lot of difficult percentages, but you certainly ought to remember that it's a 75 percent chance that you lose only one trick holding the ace-jack-ten if you finesse twice. Not only that, but in duplicate you should remember to play all the big hands the same way everyone else does.

STANLEY: I start out thinking I'm smarter than everyone else, but evidence to the contrary keeps mounting up! Twenty-nine pairs bid and made the small slam, but the creepiest result was +2210 for a *grand slam* bid and made in spades.

Up to now, after eleven hands, I've only lost us a total of 6½ match points.

KANTAR: Don't abuse yourself. My bidding was lousy. Go back to Board I, 9. You earned us a top by making a well-reasoned call that a great many players might have missed.

East-West vulnerable
North dealer (I, 9)

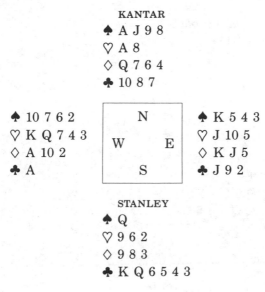

KANTAR
♠ A J 9 8
♡ A 8
◇ Q 7 6 4
♣ 10 8 7

♠ 10 7 6 2
♡ K Q 7 4 3
◇ A 10 2
♣ A

N
W E
S

♠ K 5 4 3
♡ J 10 5
◇ K J 5
♣ J 9 2

STANLEY
♠ Q
♡ 9 6 2
◇ 9 8 3
♣ K Q 6 5 4 3

The bidding:

NORTH	EAST	SOUTH	WEST
Pass	Pass	Pass	1 ♡
Double	1 NT	Pass!	Pass
Pass			

STANLEY: Occasionally I stumble in. I reasoned that you probably had the spades for your double, and I couldn't stand hearing a spade bid from you. Also, you implied tolerance for the minors, so I was quite sanguine about bringing in the club suit for a nice set. Fortunately I was lucky enough to lead the five of clubs, not the king. We beat them one trick for + 100.

KANTAR: That's how you get points in duplicate, doing the right thing at the right time. So we got 12 on the board instead of the 6½ other North-South pairs made defending against three hearts for − 140. You're only 1 match point to the bad!

CONFLICT! 161

STANLEY: Cherish the memory. It won't be long now! I dumped another five on this one!

North-South vulnerable
East dealer (I, 18)

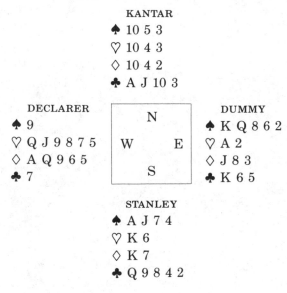

KANTAR
♠ 10 5 3
♡ 10 4 3
◇ 10 4 2
♣ A J 10 3

DECLARER
♠ 9
♡ Q J 9 8 7 5
◇ A Q 9 6 5
♣ 7

DUMMY
♠ K Q 8 6 2
♡ A 2
◇ J 8 3
♣ K 6 5

STANLEY
♠ A J 7 4
♡ K 6
◇ K 7
♣ Q 9 8 4 2

The bidding:

EAST	WEST
1 ♠	2 ♡
2 ♠	3 ◇
3 ♡	4 ♡
All pass	

STANLEY: Eddie led the ace of clubs, followed by a spade. Declarer put up the queen of spades in dummy, overtaken by my ace. Now what? I had one certain trump trick, as long as I didn't lead hearts myself. The lead of a black card would give declarer one or two sluffs plus an entry to the board he might not be able to make himself. What should I do?

KANTAR: Not what you did! This is a fairly common situation. You know you have set up cards upon which declarer can discard losers from his hand. Those tricks belong to him and there's nothing you can do about it. But how important are those discards apt to be? On the bidding you knew declarer to have a red two-suiter. And after my ace of clubs was played, you knew every high card in declarer's hand—after all, you were looking at all the rest in hand and dummy.

You led a diamond, explaining later that you knew your king was finessable, anyway. You considered it a neutral lead, but in this case being neutral was siding with the enemy. I know it's asking a great deal to expect you to visualize as far down in a suit as the *ten,* but put yourself in declarer's position and explain how you would have played the diamond suit if you'd been he?

STANLEY: I dunno. It's not easy. But the declarer said he was going to finesse the queen and then play to drop the king.

KANTAR: Ha, ha! Ho, ho! He felt sorry for you. He wanted you to be happy when the next pair came to the table. He wanted you in a good mood when facing *his* competition. Now that it's all over, we both know that one out of four East-West pairs went down at four hearts. Maybe your black-suit lead would have given declarer a chance to join the minority; anyone leading the jack of diamonds from the board would later lose a trick to the ten.

STANLEY: OK, I confess. With your opening lead we might have set them. Down another batch of match points, for the difference on this board between their game and setting them was 5 match points.

It's not often in duplicate that a lesson once learned comes right back at you on the very next board, but a similar problem came up on Board I, 19, and guess what: I blew it again!

East-West vulnerable
South dealer (I, 19)

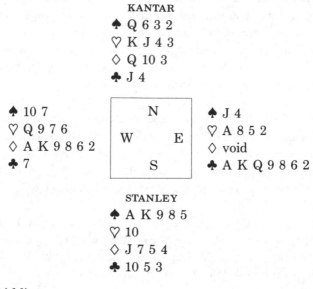

KANTAR
♠ Q 6 3 2
♡ K J 4 3
◇ Q 10 3
♣ J 4

♠ 10 7
♡ Q 9 7 6
◇ A K 9 8 6 2
♣ 7

♠ J 4
♡ A 8 5 2
◇ void
♣ A K Q 9 8 6 2

STANLEY
♠ A K 9 8 5
♡ 10
◇ J 7 5 4
♣ 10 5 3

The bidding:

WEST	EAST
2 ◇ (weak)	3 ♣
3 ♡	4 ♡
All pass	

Eddie led a small spade, I took my ace and king and then sweated for a return. The bidding had been unorthodox. A minor suit preemptive bid generally denies a four-card major, but here they were in a heart game! It occurred to me to inhibit a cross-ruff, so I led a heart!

KANTAR: A stab in the back! My own partner! Have you never heard of forcing the opponent to trump?

STANLEY: Yes, but I've also been taught never to give declarer a ruff-sluff.

KANTAR: Good advice for beginners, but you're a grown man now! When declarer has nothing but winners in his side suits, a ruff-sluff does him no good and might very well do him harm —as in this hand. If you'd given it any thought, you'd have known I had four trumps. By forcing him with a spade lead, he'd have had to decide which hand he wanted to be shortened, and no discard would do him any good. We set them one, but only because declarer misplayed the hand. Had you played a third spade like a human being, he would have had to play the hand with mirrors to hold it to one down and most certainly would have gone down at least two.

STANLEY: Horrendous! We earned 7 match points by setting them one, but we'd have scored 11 by setting them two.

We didn't realize it then, but most of our troubles were over. It wasn't till we came to Board I, 29 that you muttered a modest criticism of my play. In a way it was quite trivial, but it sharply points up the difference between the way an expert and an inexperienced player attacks a hand.

Both vulnerable
North dealer (I, 29)

KANTAR
♠ K 5 2
♡ A K 8 4
◇ 3
♣ K 9 8 7 4

♠ A 7
♡ 10 7 5
◇ K J 8 4 2
♣ A 5 3

N
W E
S

♠ J 6
♡ J 9 6 3 2
◇ A 6 5
♣ J 10 2

STANLEY
♠ Q 10 9 8 4 3
♡ Q
◇ Q 10 9 7
♣ Q 6

The bidding:

NORTH	EAST	SOUTH	WEST
1 ♣	Pass	1 ♠	2 ◇
2 ♠	Pass	4 ♠	All pass

The opening lead was the five of hearts. After West had bid two diamonds, vulnerable, that should have told me a great deal about the hand. In any event, I won in hand with the queen and led a trump. West took the ace and returned a trump. I won on the board with the king and dropped two diamonds on the ace-king of hearts. I gave up a diamond and a club to make my game.

KANTAR: Fair enough for rubber bridge players and the rabble. Fifty-three of the seventy-eight declarers who played the hand made four. (Not everyone bid game on this hand, by the way. You deserve some credit for that!) Fifteen players made five, although only seven of them had bid game.

What you should do is give the opponents a chance to go wrong.

West bid diamonds, but didn't lead them. He obviously doesn't hold both top honors. In order to have entered the bidding vulnerable, he probably has both black aces. If he does, why not tease him a little by immediately leading a small club toward your king? With those hearts sitting in dummy, he might be afraid you can discard a losing club, so he'll very likely go in with his ace. But if he ducks the club, you win with the king and discard your queen of clubs on the ace of hearts. You can then make five the way the cards lie by ruffing a club and leading either a diamond or a trump.

I can't say that your play of this hand actually cost us anything, since if West played perfectly, he'd have two chances to wake up and lead diamonds. That doesn't excuse you, however, from failing to make the most of your opportunities. Doing everything right doesn't always guarantee you top scores, but over the long haul it will make the difference between winning and losing.

STANLEY: I not only didn't think of putting the pressure on West, but it didn't occur to me that such a baggy assortment as that club suit could be established.

KANTAR: For shame! *Any* time you have a five-card suit in one hand, you should give thought to establishing it. Take a look at this deal from the Boston-Los Angeles Intercity match during the 1970 Summer Nationals.

Team-of-four
Nobody vulnerable
East dealer

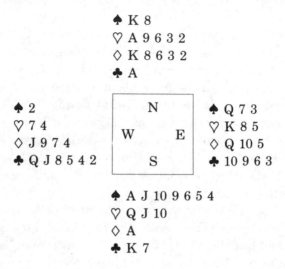

                    ♠ K 8
                    ♡ A 9 6 3 2
                    ◇ K 8 6 3 2
                    ♣ A

♠ 2   N   ♠ Q 7 3
♡ 7 4   ♡ K 8 5
◇ J 9 7 4   W   E   ◇ Q 10 5
♣ Q J 8 5 4 2   S   ♣ 10 9 6 3

                    ♠ A J 10 9 6 5 4
                    ♡ Q J 10
                    ◇ A
                    ♣ K 7

The bidding:

SOUTH	NORTH
1 ♠	2 ♡
3 ♠	4 NT
5 ♡	5 NT
6 ◇	6 ♠
All pass	

Both Wests opened the queen of clubs, and the fact that both
Don Krauss of Los Angeles and Ken Barbour of Boston made
the slam the same way is important. They won in dummy and
came to their hands with the ace of diamonds. They led a spade
to the king and ruffed a small diamond in the closed hand. They
ruffed their good king of clubs on the table and ruffed another
small diamond. Now the ace of spades was cashed and a trick
conceded to the queen of spades. The ace of hearts provided
an entry to the board to discard two hearts on dummy's estab-

GAMESMAN BRIDGE

lished diamonds. This hand is perfect proof of the value of setting up what you call a "baggy" side suit—this time of only six cards distributed 5-1—and a further demonstration of expert reluctance to take finesses.

STANLEY: OK. From now on, I'll think before I play, count, count, count, and regard finesses like flies in my soup.

When our first session was over, we discovered we had come in seventh over-all with a score of 189 match points. I felt confident we would do better the next day, for I believed I had gotten all my worst mistakes out of my system. Eddie was calm in the face of this good result, no doubt because he figured we'd have had a much higher score if I hadn't dribbled away so many crucial tricks.

KANTAR: I didn't think you had done too badly. You had trouble on six boards, but on twenty you played well. In that many hands you have to make about four hundred decisions in bidding and play. Your eight or ten mistakes were unfortunate, but most of the time you seemed to remember to make the right plays. In duplicate the rewards for playing good, sound bridge are never as obvious as the penalties you get for making mistakes. For example, in this hand you remembered your lessons very well, and though your opening lead gained us no more than three or four match points, several such gains mount up in the end:

Neither vulnerable
East dealer (I, 14)

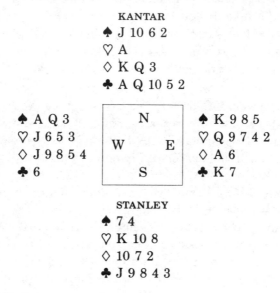

KANTAR
♠ J 10 6 2
♡ A
◇ K Q 3
♣ A Q 10 5 2

♠ A Q 3
♡ J 6 5 3
◇ J 9 8 5 4
♣ 6

N
W   E
S

♠ K 9 8 5
♡ Q 9 7 4 2
◇ A 6
♣ K 7

STANLEY
♠ 7 4
♡ K 10 8
◇ 10 7 2
♣ J 9 8 4 3

The bidding:

EAST	SOUTH	WEST	NORTH
Pass	Pass	Pass	1 ♣
1 ♡	Pass	2 ♡	Double
Pass	3 ♣	3 ♡	All Pass

Holding a trump control, you quite properly thought you could get a ruffing trick, so instead of leading the suit I bid, you led the seven of spades. Declarer won in dummy and started trumps. I won and continued spades. On declarer's trump continuation, you won the king and put me in with the ace of clubs. My spade return gave you the ruff, and we later had to win a diamond. Down one for eight match points.

STANLEY: The following afternoon we played East-West in

Section C, competing against a new set of adversaries who the previous afternoon had played East-West in Section D. I was encouraged to see that one of the pairs opposing us had scored exactly 100 match points fewer than we had the day before. With a 29 percent game to their credit, I didn't anticipate any trouble from *that* pair!

The very first hand produced a lesson in tactics.

North-South vulnerable
North dealer (II, 5)

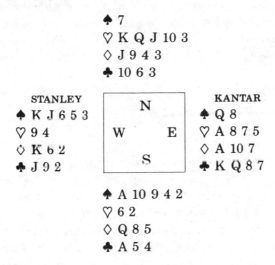

♠ 7
♡ K Q J 10 3
◇ J 9 4 3
♣ 10 6 3

STANLEY
♠ K J 6 5 3
♡ 9 4
◇ K 6 2
♣ J 9 2

KANTAR
♠ Q 8
♡ A 8 7 5
◇ A 10 7
♣ K Q 8 7

♠ A 10 9 4 2
♡ 6 2
◇ Q 8 5
♣ A 5 4

The bidding:

EAST	WEST
1 NT	2 ♣
2 ♡	2 NT
All pass	

Eddie opened one notrump and I had the values for a raise to two, but if he had a four-card spade suit, we should be in game even if his had been a minimal opening. When he showed a four-card heart suit, I converted to two notrump, resisting the urge to say three. Eddie made four, and I kicked myself.

KANTAR: A waste of shoe leather. Bidding a shaky game is all right in rubber bridge or team play, but seldom in duplicate—particularly at the beginning of a session. Later on, if you know you're losing, you might shoot for a top score on a hand such as this.

STANLEY: But I always expect you to wring an extra trick out of every hand.

KANTAR: Thanks. But it is relatively unimportant to bid a game in a situation like this. We got 8½ match points for scoring +180—a better than average result on a hand that in game could go down. (It went down one out of four times it was played.)

STANLEY: I wish I'd remembered that later on in this event!

KANTAR: Incidentally, once you trot out Stayman holding a *five*-card major, you should bid the suit even though I deny four. After all, I might have three-card support for your suit and a 5-3 spade fit might be a better contract than notrump.

STANLEY: Next we came up against the pair who had scored only 89 match points in the previous session. On the first hand they played a sound notrump game that eighty other teams played in spades. On the next they bid another game in notrump for an easy make. Two out of three pairs with the same cards stopped short of game! They beat us for 20½ match points out of a possible 24, making close to 10 percent of the total 219½ match points they made over the full fifty-two boards!

KANTAR: Stop moaning and groaning! We were fixed, but not unreasonably. It was nothing compared to what you did to our opponents on the next board!

Both vulnerable
North dealer (II, 13)

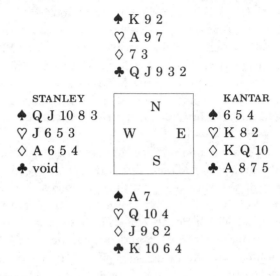

♠ K 9 2
♡ A 9 7
♢ 7 3
♣ Q J 9 3 2

STANLEY
♠ Q J 10 8 3
♡ J 6 5 3
♢ A 6 5 4
♣ void

KANTAR
♠ 6 5 4
♡ K 8 2
♢ K Q 10
♣ A 8 7 5

♠ A 7
♡ Q 10 4
♢ J 9 8 2
♣ K 10 6 4

The bidding

NORTH	EAST	SOUTH	WEST
Pass	Pass	Pass	2 ♠!!!
Pass	2 NT	Pass	3 ♡
Pass	3 NT	—	All pass

STANLEY: By way of apology, no mere explanation of this bidding being possible, let me say this: Although holding only eight high-card points, I felt my distribution and nine cards in the major suits called for an opening bid. Being afraid Eddie would think I had a *legitimate* opening if I bid one spade, I thought to warn him off by bidding *two*. His two notrump asked me to show a feature if I had a *maximum number* of high-card points for my bid. I didn't think I had the shape to leave it in notrump, so I bid hearts, hoping he'd be enough of a mind reader to know my feature was *length*, not the ace of hearts.

When he bid three notrump, I realized I had done enough damage on this hand and passed.

KANTAR: It never occurred to me that you were so unfamiliar with the weak two-bid. Since it is unnecessary to use it as preemptive in fourth position, it usually shows 10-12 high-card points and a good six-card suit. Next time you have a lousy hand in fourth seat, do me a big favor—pass!

The defense was something to behold. If I hadn't seen those fellows before, I would have sworn they owed me money and were trying to buy me off!

South led a diamond which I won with the ten. I led a spade, and North won the king, dutifully returning his partner's suit in spite of the club void in dummy and his own attractive holding in that suit. I won the king of diamonds and played a second spade, which South was forced to win with the ace. Doggedly he played a third round of diamonds to my queen. Now I was home. I ran my spades, cashed my ace of diamonds, and led up to my king of hearts. North captured the trick with his ace of hearts and had a brain wave, but his club lead was too late. I came to nine tricks: three spades, four diamonds, a club, and a heart. But please don't ever do that to me again. The truth of the matter is that they had a better play for nine tricks with their cards than we had with ours, but once they each decided that clubs weren't part of the game, I was able to make this absurd contract.

STANLEY: I'm glad I brought you! You were not only top on the board in our section, but the only one of seventy-eight players to bid and make game. If I had passed the hand out, we'd have taken 4 match points; instead we took 12!

KANTAR: We! I keep saying bridge is a partnership game, but this is ridiculous. You can figure the odds against making three notrump on that hand at 77 to 1. That's a lousy risk for a mere 8 match points. I absolutely refuse to give you credit for bad bids that turn out well. Also, you've got to consider how destructive a bid like that is to partnership morale. If I weren't twice the man of iron you claim I am, I'd have been an empty shell for the next half-dozen boards.

STANLEY: I didn't realize it at the time, but we had passed the halfway mark with a fairly good game.

KANTAR: Perhaps I should have encouraged you. Difficult as it is to understand the bidding of a new partner, it's much more difficult to know what to say to him during a match. Some people blow up if you tell them they have a good game. You seemed relaxed enough to me.

STANLEY: That wasn't relaxation, that was numbness. Anyway, the next hand brought out the worst in me, showing up what I consider to be my most glaring weakness—inability to cope with low-level contracts.

East-West vulnerable
South dealer (II, 3)

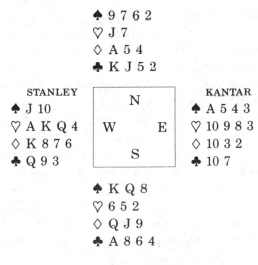

```
                 ♠ 9 7 6 2
                 ♡ J 7
                 ◇ A 5 4
                 ♣ K J 5 2

    STANLEY          N          KANTAR
    ♠ J 10                      ♠ A 5 4 3
    ♡ A K Q 4     W       E     ♡ 10 9 8 3
    ◇ K 8 7 6                   ◇ 10 3 2
    ♣ Q 9 3          S          ♣ 10 7

                 ♠ K Q 8
                 ♡ 6 5 2
                 ◇ Q J 9
                 ♣ A 8 6 4
```

The bidding:

WEST	EAST
1 ♡	2 ♡
All pass	

The opening lead was the deuce of spades. I could be sure of four hearts, a spade, and a club ruff in dummy for six tricks. Down two vulnerable would be a disaster, but with only nineteen high-card points between us, I felt that going down one might get us a good board. (How right I was! It would have been worth 9 match points!) I ducked the first spade, taken by South's queen, followed by a return of the king. I won with dummy's ace and made an immediate shot to make the king of diamonds. It lost to the ace and North forced me in spades. I pulled trumps and continued diamonds, but there was no way to get to my thirteenth diamond after they had taken their top tricks and I ruffed my last club on the board. I wound up taking the six tricks I counted in the beginning.

KANTAR: This is the sort of hand where you should defer to the enemy. Let your opponents make all the mistakes. Lead the ten of clubs at trick three, and see what happens. Maybe they will break diamonds from the wrong side of the table. Maybe the ten of clubs will force out the king or ace and they will return a club, making your queen good for a possible diamond discard. In any event, you cannot draw trumps and leave that fourth spade on the board. Once you have no more trumps in your hand, that spade is a sure loser.

STANLEY: At the time, I thought kicking that hand was the last straw. But I hadn't reckoned on the final round! We came up against a former partner of mine, and he paid me back for all the times I had let him down in the past. He flattened us flat.

KANTAR: Correction. You flattened yourself flat. You came to the table discouraged over what you thought was a bad game. You were thinking about past mistakes, even though you had no way of knowing how costly they might have been. Duplicate is a funny game—sometimes when you think you've scored a zero, half a dozen other players in your seat have made the same mistake to give you an average score. At any rate, the time to worry about that is *definitely not* before you play the last round.

If we had beaten our last opponents as badly as they beat us, we'd have finished in the money.

STANLEY: I confess I was anything but cool! The pace had quickened, I was tired, and had lost control. Reason fled, and I finished out the game on raw emotion. At that, we had an acceptable game. We scored $161\frac{1}{2}$ match points on the final session for an overall of $350\frac{1}{2}$. We ended in a four-way tie for twenty-first place, 14 match points out of the money, and only 35 out of first place. Since I counted 45 match points worth of personal goofs, I was ashamed to look Eddie in the eye. After all, if we had won, what a great proof of his teaching ability it would have been!

KANTAR: You're a hard loser, Stanley, old friend. If I staked my reputation on the results of a two-session pairs event, I'd have long since gone back to the harness factory.

STANLEY: You ought to be proud that you were able to teach me so well.

KANTAR: I think I missed something. When you first came to me you told me about your bad leads and shaky play of the dummy, so I concentrated on counting, and drawing inferences, and communication—the *play*. But after playing with you I've decided that most of your faults were in *bidding*. Why didn't you tell me you were such a bad bidder?

STANLEY: I didn't know. But we can fix that easy enough. Teach me to bid, we'll write another book, and play in another tournament sometime.

KANTAR: (censored!)

A PERSONAL WORD FROM MELVIN POWERS, PUBLISHER, WILSHIRE BOOK COMPANY

My goal is to publish interesting, informative, and inspirational books. You can help me to accomplish this by sending me your answers to the following questions:

Did you enjoy reading this book? Why?

What ideas in the book impressed you most? Have you applied them to your daily life? How?

Is there a chapter that could serve as a theme for an entire book? Explain.

Would you like to read similar books? What additional information would you like them to contain?

If you have an idea for a book, I would welcome discussing it with you. If you have a manuscript in progress, write or call me concerning possible publication.

Melvin Powers
12015 Sherman Road
North Hollywood, California 91605

(818) 765-8579

MELVIN POWERS SELF-IMPROVEMENT LIBRARY

ASTROLOGY

___ ASTROLOGY: HOW TO CHART YOUR HOROSCOPE *Max Heindel*   5.00
___ ASTROLOGY AND SEXUAL ANALYSIS *Morris C. Goodman*   5.00
___ ASTROLOGY AND YOU *Carroll Righter*   5.00
___ ASTROLOGY MADE EASY *Astarte*   5.00
___ ASTROLOGY, ROMANCE, YOU AND THE STARS *Anthony Norvell*   5.00
___ MY WORLD OF ASTROLOGY *Sydney Omarr*   7.00
___ THOUGHT DIAL *Sydney Omarr*   7.00
___ WHAT THE STARS REVEAL ABOUT THE MEN IN YOUR LIFE *Thelma White*   3.00

BRIDGE

___ BRIDGE BIDDING MADE EASY *Edwin B. Kantar*   10.00
___ BRIDGE CONVENTIONS *Edwin B. Kantar*   10.00
___ COMPETITIVE BIDDING IN MODERN BRIDGE *Edgar Kaplan*   7.00
___ DEFENSIVE BRIDGE PLAY COMPLETE *Edwin B. Kantar*   15.00
___ GAMESMAN BRIDGE–PLAY BETTER WITH KANTAR *Edwin B. Kantar*   7.00
___ HOW TO IMPROVE YOUR BRIDGE *Alfred Sheinwold*   7.00
___ IMPROVING YOUR BIDDING SKILLS *Edwin B. Kantar*   7.00
___ INTRODUCTION TO DECLARER'S PLAY *Edwin B. Kantar*   7.00
___ INTRODUCTION TO DEFENDER'S PLAY *Edwin B. Kantar*   7.00
___ KANTAR FOR THE DEFENSE *Edwin B. Kantar*   7.00
___ KANTAR FOR THE DEFENSE VOLUME 2 *Edwin B. Kantar*   7.00
___ TEST YOUR BRIDGE PLAY *Edwin B. Kantar*   7.00
___ VOLUME 2–TEST YOUR BRIDGE PLAY *Edwin B. Kantar*   7.00
___ WINNING DECLARER PLAY *Dorothy Hayden Truscott*   7.00

BUSINESS, STUDY & REFERENCE

___ BRAINSTORMING *Charles Clark*   7.00
___ CONVERSATION MADE EASY *Elliot Russell*   5.00
___ EXAM SECRET *Dennis B. Jackson*   5.00
___ FIX-IT BOOK *Arthur Symons*   2.00
___ HOW TO DEVELOP A BETTER SPEAKING VOICE *M. Hellier*   4.00
___ HOW TO SAVE 50% ON GAS & CAR EXPENSES *Ken Stansbie*   5.00
___ HOW TO SELF-PUBLISH YOUR BOOK & MAKE IT A BEST SELLER *Melvin Powers*   20.00
___ INCREASE YOUR LEARNING POWER *Geoffrey A. Dudley*   3.00
___ PRACTICAL GUIDE TO BETTER CONCENTRATION *Melvin Powers*   5.00
___ 7 DAYS TO FASTER READING *William S. Schaill*   5.00
___ SONGWRITERS' RHYMING DICTIONARY *Jane Shaw Whitfield*   10.00
___ SPELLING MADE EASY *Lester D. Basch & Dr. Milton Finkelstein*   3.00
___ STUDENT'S GUIDE TO BETTER GRADES *J. A. Rickard*   3.00
___ TEST YOURSELF–FIND YOUR HIDDEN TALENT *Jack Shafer*   3.00
___ YOUR WILL & WHAT TO DO ABOUT IT *Attorney Samuel G. Kling*   5.00

CALLIGRAPHY

___ ADVANCED CALLIGRAPHY *Katherine Jeffares*   7.00
___ CALLIGRAPHY–THE ART OF BEAUTIFUL WRITING *Katherine Jeffares*   7.00
___ CALLIGRAPHY FOR FUN & PROFIT *Anne Leptich & Jacque Evans*   7.00
___ CALLIGRAPHY MADE EASY *Tina Serafini*   7.00

CHESS & CHECKERS

___ BEGINNER'S GUIDE TO WINNING CHESS *Fred Reinfeld*   5.00
___ CHESS IN TEN EASY LESSONS *Larry Evans*   5.00
___ CHESS MADE EASY *Milton L. Hanauer*   5.00
___ CHESS PROBLEMS FOR BEGINNERS *Edited by Fred Reinfeld*   5.00
___ CHESS TACTICS FOR BEGINNERS *Edited by Fred Reinfeld*   5.00

___ HOW TO WIN AT CHECKERS *Fred Reinfeld*	5.00
___ 1001 BRILLIANT WAYS TO CHECKMATE *Fred Reinfeld*	7.00
___ 1001 WINNING CHESS SACRIFICES & COMBINATIONS *Fred Reinfeld*	7.00

COOKERY & HERBS

___ CULPEPER'S HERBAL REMEDIES *Dr. Nicholas Culpeper*	5.00
___ FAST GOURMET COOKBOOK *Poppy Cannon*	2.50
___ HEALING POWER OF HERBS *May Bethel*	5.00
___ HEALING POWER OF NATURAL FOODS *May Bethel*	5.00
___ HERBS FOR HEALTH—HOW TO GROW & USE THEM *Louise Evans Doole*	5.00
___ HOME GARDEN COOKBOOK—DELICIOUS NATURAL FOOD RECIPES *Ken Kraft*	3.00
___ MEATLESS MEAL GUIDE *Tomi Ryan & James H. Ryan, M.D.*	4.00
___ VEGETABLE GARDENING FOR BEGINNERS *Hugh Wiberg*	2.00
___ VEGETABLES FOR TODAY'S GARDENS *R. Milton Carleton*	2.00
___ VEGETARIAN COOKERY *Janet Walker*	7.00
___ VEGETARIAN COOKING MADE EASY & DELECTABLE *Veronica Vezza*	3.00
___ VEGETARIAN DELIGHTS—A HAPPY COOKBOOK FOR HEALTH *K. R. Mer*	2.00
___ VEGETARIAN GOURMET COOKBOOK *Joyce McKinnel*	3.00

GAMBLING & POKER

___ HOW TO WIN AT DICE GAMES *Skip Frey*	3.00
___ HOW TO WIN AT POKER *Terence Reese & Anthony T. Watkins*	7.00
___ WINNING AT CRAPS *Dr. Lloyd T. Commins*	5.00
___ WINNING AT GIN *Chester Wander & Cy Rice*	3.00
___ WINNING AT POKER—AN EXPERT'S GUIDE *John Archer*	5.00
___ WINNING AT 21—AN EXPERT'S GUIDE *John Archer*	7.00
___ WINNING POKER SYSTEMS *Norman Zadeh*	3.00

HEALTH

___ BEE POLLEN *Lynda Lyngheim & Jack Scagnetti*	3.00
___ COPING WITH ALZHEIMER'S *Rose Oliver, Ph.D. & Francis Bock, Ph.D.*	10.00
___ DR. LINDNER'S POINT SYSTEM FOOD PROGRAM *Peter G. Lindner, M.D.*	2.00
___ HELP YOURSELF TO BETTER SIGHT *Margaret Darst Corbett*	7.00
___ HOW YOU CAN STOP SMOKING PERMANENTLY *Ernest Caldwell*	5.00
___ MIND OVER PLATTER *Peter G. Lindner, M.D.*	5.00
___ NATURE'S WAY TO NUTRITION & VIBRANT HEALTH *Robert J. Scrutton*	3.00
___ NEW CARBOHYDRATE DIET COUNTER *Patti Lopez-Pereira*	2.00
___ REFLEXOLOGY *Dr. Maybelle Segal*	5.00
___ REFLEXOLOGY FOR GOOD HEALTH *Anna Kaye & Don C. Matchan*	7.00
___ 30 DAYS TO BEAUTIFUL LEGS *Dr. Marc Selner*	3.00
___ YOU CAN LEARN TO RELAX *Dr. Samuel Gutwirth*	3.00

HOBBIES

___ BEACHCOMBING FOR BEGINNERS *Norman Hickin*	2.00
___ BLACKSTONE'S MODERN CARD TRICKS *Harry Blackstone*	5.00
___ BLACKSTONE'S SECRETS OF MAGIC *Harry Blackstone*	5.00
___ COIN COLLECTING FOR BEGINNERS *Burton Hobson & Fred Reinfeld*	7.00
___ ENTERTAINING WITH ESP *Tony 'Doc' Shiels*	2.00
___ 400 FASCINATING MAGIC TRICKS YOU CAN DO *Howard Thurston*	7.00
___ HOW I TURN JUNK INTO FUN AND PROFIT *Sari*	3.00
___ HOW TO WRITE A HIT SONG & SELL IT *Tommy Boyce*	7.00
___ JUGGLING MADE EASY *Rudolf Dittrich*	3.00
___ MAGIC FOR ALL AGES *Walter Gibson*	4.00
___ MAGIC MADE EASY *Byron Wels*	2.00
___ STAMP COLLECTING FOR BEGINNERS *Burton Hobson*	3.00

HORSE PLAYER'S WINNING GUIDES

___ BETTING HORSES TO WIN *Les Conklin*	7.00
___ ELIMINATE THE LOSERS *Bob McKnight*	5.00
___ HOW TO PICK WINNING HORSES *Bob McKnight*	5.00

___ HOW TO WIN AT THE RACES *Sam (The Genius) Lewin*	5.00
___ HOW YOU CAN BEAT THE RACES *Jack Kavanaqh*	5.00
___ MAKING MONEY AT THE RACES *David Barr*	5.00
___ PAYDAY AT THE RACES *Les Conklin*	5.00
___ SMART HANDICAPPING MADE EASY *William Bauman*	5.00
___ SUCCESS AT THE HARNESS RACES *Barry Meadow*	5.00

HUMOR

___ HOW TO FLATTEN YOUR TUSH *Coach Marge Reardon*	2.00
___ HOW TO MAKE LOVE TO YOURSELF *Ron Stevens & Joy Grdnic*	3.00
___ JOKE TELLER'S HANDBOOK *Bob Orben*	7.00
___ JOKES FOR ALL OCCASIONS *Al Schock*	5.00
___ 2,000 NEW LAUGHS FOR SPEAKERS *Bob Orben*	7.00
___ 2,400 JOKES TO BRIGHTEN YOUR SPEECHES *Robert Orben*	7.00
___ 2,500 JOKES TO START 'EM LAUGHING *Bob Orben*	7.00

HYPNOTISM

___ ADVANCED TECHNIQUES OF HYPNOSIS *Melvin Powers*	3.00
___ CHILDBIRTH WITH HYPNOSIS *William S. Kroger, M.D.*	5.00
___ HOW TO SOLVE YOUR SEX PROBLEMS WITH SELF-HYPNOSIS *Frank S. Caprio, M.D.*	5.00
___ HOW TO STOP SMOKING THRU SELF-HYPNOSIS *Leslie M. LeCron*	3.00
___ HOW YOU CAN BOWL BETTER USING SELF-HYPNOSIS *Jack Heise*	4.00
___ HOW YOU CAN PLAY BETTER GOLF USING SELF-HYPNOSIS *Jack Heise*	3.00
___ HYPNOSIS AND SELF-HYPNOSIS *Bernard Hollander, M.D.*	5.00
___ HYPNOTISM *(Originally published in 1893) Carl Sextus*	5.00
___ HYPNOTISM MADE EASY *Dr. Ralph Winn*	5.00
___ HYPNOTISM MADE PRACTICAL *Louis Orton*	5.00
___ HYPNOTISM REVEALED *Melvin Powers*	3.00
___ HYPNOTISM TODAY *Leslie LeCron and Jean Bordeaux, Ph.D.*	5.00
___ MODERN HYPNOSIS *Lesley Kuhn & Salvatore Russo, Ph.D.*	5.00
___ NEW CONCEPTS OF HYPNOSIS *Bernard C. Gindes, M.D.*	10.00
___ NEW SELF-HYPNOSIS *Paul Adams*	7.00
___ POST-HYPNOTIC INSTRUCTIONS—SUGGESTIONS FOR THERAPY *Arnold Furst*	5.00
___ PRACTICAL GUIDE TO SELF-HYPNOSIS *Melvin Powers*	3.00
___ PRACTICAL HYPNOTISM *Philip Magonet, M.D.*	3.00
___ SECRETS OF HYPNOTISM *S. J. Van Pelt, M.D.*	5.00
___ SELF-HYPNOSIS—A CONDITIONED-RESPONSE TECHNIQUE *Laurence Sparks*	7.00
___ SELF-HYPNOSIS—ITS THEORY, TECHNIQUE & APPLICATION *Melvin Powers*	3.00
___ THERAPY THROUGH HYPNOSIS *Edited by Raphael H. Rhodes*	5.00

JUDAICA

___ SERVICE OF THE HEART *Evelyn Garfiel, Ph.D.*	10.00
___ STORY OF ISRAEL IN COINS *Jean & Maurice Gould*	2.00
___ STORY OF ISRAEL IN STAMPS *Maxim & Gabriel Shamir*	1.00
___ TONGUE OF THE PROPHETS *Robert St. John*	7.00

JUST FOR WOMEN

___ COSMOPOLITAN'S GUIDE TO MARVELOUS MEN Foreword by *Helen Gurley Brown*	3.00
___ COSMOPOLITAN'S HANG-UP HANDBOOK Foreword by *Helen Gurley Brown*	4.00
___ COSMOPOLITAN'S LOVE BOOK—A GUIDE TO ECSTASY IN BED	7.00
___ COSMOPOLITAN'S NEW ETIQUETTE GUIDE Foreword by *Helen Gurley Brown*	4.00
___ I AM A COMPLEAT WOMAN *Doris Hagopian & Karen O'Connor Sweeney*	3.00
___ JUST FOR WOMEN—A GUIDE TO THE FEMALE BODY *Richard E. Sand, M.D.*	5.00
___ NEW APPROACHES TO SEX IN MARRIAGE *John E. Eichenlaub, M.D.*	3.00
___ SEXUALLY ADEQUATE FEMALE *Frank S. Caprio, M.D.*	3.00
___ SEXUALLY FULFILLED WOMAN *Dr. Rachel Copelan*	5.00

MARRIAGE, SEX & PARENTHOOD

____ ABILITY TO LOVE *Dr. Allan Fromme* — 7.0

____ GUIDE TO SUCCESSFUL MARRIAGE *Drs. Albert Ellis & Robert Harper* — 7.0

____ HOW TO RAISE AN EMOTIONALLY HEALTHY, HAPPY CHILD *Albert Ellis, Ph.D.* — 7.0

____ PARENT SURVIVAL TRAINING *Marvin Silverman, Ed.D. & David Lustig, Ph.D.* — 10.0

____ SEX WITHOUT GUILT *Albert Ellis, Ph.D.* — 5.0

____ SEXUALLY ADEQUATE MALE *Frank S. Caprio, M.D.* — 3.0

____ SEXUALLY FULFILLED MAN *Dr. Rachel Copelan* — 5.0

____ STAYING IN LOVE *Dr. Norton F. Kristy* — 7.0

MELVIN POWERS' MAIL ORDER LIBRARY

____ HOW TO GET RICH IN MAIL ORDER *Melvin Powers* — 20.0

____ HOW TO WRITE A GOOD ADVERTISEMENT *Victor O. Schwab* — 20.0

____ MAIL ORDER MADE EASY *J. Frank Brumbaugh* — 20.0

METAPHYSICS & OCCULT

____ CONCENTRATION—A GUIDE TO MENTAL MASTERY *Mouni Sadhu* — 7.00

____ EXTRA-TERRESTRIAL INTELLIGENCE—THE FIRST ENCOUNTER — 6.00

____ FORTUNE TELLING WITH CARDS *P. Foli* — 5.00

____ HOW TO INTERPRET DREAMS, OMENS & FORTUNE TELLING SIGNS *Gettings* — 5.00

____ HOW TO UNDERSTAND YOUR DREAMS *Geoffrey A. Dudley* — 5.00

____ IN DAYS OF GREAT PEACE *Mouni Sadhu* — 3.00

____ MAGICIAN—HIS TRAINING AND WORK *W. E. Butler* — 5.00

____ MEDITATION *Mouni Sadhu* — 10.00

____ MODERN NUMEROLOGY *Morris C. Goodman* — 5.00

____ NUMEROLOGY—ITS FACTS AND SECRETS *Ariel Yvon Taylor* — 5.00

____ NUMEROLOGY MADE EASY *W. Mykian* — 5.00

____ PALMISTRY MADE EASY *Fred Gettings* — 5.00

____ PALMISTRY MADE PRACTICAL *Elizabeth Daniels Squire* — 7.00

____ PALMISTRY SECRETS REVEALED *Henry Frith* — 4.00

____ PROPHECY IN OUR TIME *Martin Ebon* — 2.50

____ SUPERSTITION—ARE YOU SUPERSTITIOUS? *Eric Maple* — 2.00

____ TAROT *Mouni Sadhu* — 10.00

____ TAROT OF THE BOHEMIANS *Papus* — 7.00

____ WAYS TO SELF-REALIZATION *Mouni Sadhu* — 7.00

____ WITCHCRAFT, MAGIC & OCCULTISM—A FASCINATING HISTORY *W. B. Crow* — 7.00

____ WITCHCRAFT—THE SIXTH SENSE *Justine Glass* — 7.00

RECOVERY

____ KNIGHT IN RUSTY ARMOR *Robert Fisher* — 5.00

____ KNIGHT IN RUSTY ARMOR *Robert Fisher (Hard cover edition)* — 10.00

SELF-HELP & INSPIRATIONAL

____ CHARISMA—HOW TO GET "THAT SPECIAL MAGIC" *Marcia Grad* — 7.00

____ DAILY POWER FOR JOYFUL LIVING *Dr. Donald Curtis* — 7.00

____ DYNAMIC THINKING *Melvin Powers* — 5.00

____ GREATEST POWER IN THE UNIVERSE *U. S. Andersen* — 7.00

____ GROW RICH WHILE YOU SLEEP *Ben Sweetland* — 7.00

____ GROW RICH WITH YOUR MILLION DOLLAR MIND *Brian Adams* — 7.00

____ GROWTH THROUGH REASON *Albert Ellis, Ph.D.* — 7.00

____ GUIDE TO PERSONAL HAPPINESS *Albert Ellis, Ph.D. & Irving Becker, Ed.D.* — 7.00

____ HANDWRITING ANALYSIS MADE EASY *John Marley* — 7.00

____ HANDWRITING TELLS *Nadya Olyanova* — 7.00

____ HOW TO ATTRACT GOOD LUCK *A.H.Z. Carr* — 7.00

____ HOW TO DEVELOP A WINNING PERSONALITY *Martin Panzer* — 7.00

____ HOW TO DEVELOP AN EXCEPTIONAL MEMORY *Young & Gibson* — 7.00

____ HOW TO LIVE WITH A NEUROTIC *Albert Ellis, Ph.D.* — 7.00

____ HOW TO OVERCOME YOUR FEARS *M. P. Leahy, M.D.* — 3.00

____ HOW TO SUCCEED *Brian Adams* — 7.00

____ HUMAN PROBLEMS & HOW TO SOLVE THEM *Dr. Donald Curtis* — 5.00

____ I CAN *Ben Sweetland* — 8.00

___ I WILL *Ben Sweetland*		7.00
___ KNIGHT IN RUSTY ARMOR *Robert Fisher*		5.00
___ KNIGHT IN RUSTY ARMOR *Robert Fisher (Hard cover edition)*		10.00
___ LEFT-HANDED PEOPLE *Michael Barsley*		5.00
___ MAGIC IN YOUR MIND *U.S. Andersen*		10.00
___ MAGIC OF THINKING SUCCESS *Dr. David J. Schwartz*		7.00
___ MAGIC POWER OF YOUR MIND *Walter M. Germain*		7.00
___ MENTAL POWER THROUGH SLEEP SUGGESTION *Melvin Powers*		3.00
___ NEVER UNDERESTIMATE THE SELLING POWER OF A WOMAN *Dottie Walters*		7.00
___ NEW GUIDE TO RATIONAL LIVING *Albert Ellis, Ph.D. & R. Harper, Ph.D.*		7.00
___ PSYCHO-CYBERNETICS *Maxwell Maltz, M.D.*		7.00
___ PSYCHOLOGY OF HANDWRITING *Nadya Olyanova*		7.00
___ SALES CYBERNETICS *Brian Adams*		10.00
___ SCIENCE OF MIND IN DAILY LIVING *Dr. Donald Curtis*		7.00
___ SECRET OF SECRETS *U.S. Andersen*		7.00
___ SECRET POWER OF THE PYRAMIDS *U. S. Andersen*		7.00
___ SELF-THERAPY FOR THE STUTTERER *Malcolm Frazer*		3.00
___ SUCCESS-CYBERNETICS *U. S. Andersen*		7.00
___ 10 DAYS TO A GREAT NEW LIFE *William E. Edwards*		3.00
___ THINK AND GROW RICH *Napoleon Hill*		8.00
___ THREE MAGIC WORDS *U. S. Andersen*		7.00
___ TREASURY OF COMFORT *Edited by Rabbi Sidney Greenberg*		10.00
___ TREASURY OF THE ART OF LIVING *Sidney S. Greenberg*		7.00
___ WHAT YOUR HANDWRITING REVEALS *Albert E. Hughes*		4.00
___ YOUR SUBCONSCIOUS POWER *Charles M. Simmons*		7.00
___ YOUR THOUGHTS CAN CHANGE YOUR LIFE *Dr. Donald Curtis*		7.00

SPORTS

___ BICYCLING FOR FUN AND GOOD HEALTH *Kenneth E. Luther*		2.00
___ BILLIARDS—POCKET • CAROM • THREE CUSHION *Clive Cottingham, Jr.*		5.00
___ COMPLETE GUIDE TO FISHING *Vlad Evanoff*		2.00
___ HOW TO IMPROVE YOUR RACQUETBALL *Lubarsky, Kaufman & Scagnetti*		5.00
___ HOW TO WIN AT POCKET BILLIARDS *Edward D. Knuchell*		7.00
___ JOY OF WALKING *Jack Scagnetti*		3.00
___ LEARNING & TEACHING SOCCER SKILLS *Eric Worthington*		3.00
___ MOTORCYCLING FOR BEGINNERS *I.G. Edmonds*		3.00
___ RACQUETBALL FOR WOMEN *Toni Hudson, Jack Scagnetti & Vince Rondone*		3.00
___ RACQUETBALL MADE EASY *Steve Lubarsky, Rod Delson & Jack Scagnetti*		5.00
___ SECRET OF BOWLING STRIKES *Dawson Taylor*		5.00
___ SOCCER—THE GAME & HOW TO PLAY IT *Gary Rosenthal*		7.00
___ STARTING SOCCER *Edward F. Dolan, Jr.*		3.00

TENNIS LOVER'S LIBRARY

___ BEGINNER'S GUIDE TO WINNING TENNIS *Helen Hull Jacobs*		2.00
___ HOW TO BEAT BETTER TENNIS PLAYERS *Loring Fiske*		4.00
___ PSYCH YOURSELF TO BETTER TENNIS *Dr. Walter A. Luszki*		2.00
___ TENNIS FOR BEGINNERS *Dr. H. A. Murray*		2.00
___ TENNIS MADE EASY *Joel Brecheen*		5.00
___ WEEKEND TENNIS—HOW TO HAVE FUN & WIN AT THE SAME TIME *Bill Talbert*		3.00

WILSHIRE PET LIBRARY

___ DOG TRAINING MADE EASY & FUN *John W. Kellogg*		5.00
___ HOW TO BRING UP YOUR PET DOG *Kurt Unkelbach*		2.00
___ HOW TO RAISE & TRAIN YOUR PUPPY *Jeff Griffen*		5.00

The books listed above can be obtained from your book dealer or directly from Melvin Powers. When ordering, please remit $2.00 postage for the first book and 50¢ for each additional book.

Melvin Powers
12015 Sherman Road, No. Hollywood, California 91605

WILSHIRE HORSE LOVERS' LIBRARY

The books listed above can be obtained from your book dealer or directly from Melvin Powers. When ordering, please remit $2.00 postage for the first book and 50¢ for each additional book.

Melvin Powers
12015 Sherman Road, No. Hollywood, California 91605

HOW TO GET RICH IN MAIL ORDER
by Melvin Powers

How to Develop Your Mail Order Expertise 2. How to Find a Unique Product or Service
Sell 3. How to Make Money with Classified Ads 4. How to Make Money with Display Ads
The Unlimited Potential for Making Money with Direct Mail 6. How to Copycat Successful
Mail Order Operations 7. How I Created A Best Seller Using the Copycat Technique 8. How
Start and Run a Profitable Mail Order, Special Interest Book or Record Business 9. I Enjoy
Selling Books by Mail — Some of My Successful and Not-So-Successful Ads and Direct Mail
Circulars 10. Five of My Most Successful Direct Mail Pieces That Sold and Are Still Selling
Millions of Dollars Worth of Books 11. Melvin Powers' Mail Order Success Strategy — Follow
and You'll Become a Millionaire 12. How to Sell Your Products to Mail Order Companies,
Retail Outlets, Jobbers, and Fund Raisers for Maximum Distribution and Profits 13. How to
Get Free Display Ads and Publicity That Can Put You on the Road to Riches 14. How to Make
Your Advertising Copy Sizzle to Make You Wealthy 15. Questions and Answers to Help You
Get Started Making Money in Your Own Mail Order Business 16. A Personal Word from
Melvin Powers 17. How to Get Started Making Money in Mail Order. 18. Selling Products
on Television - An Exciting Challenge   8½"x11" — 352 Pages ... $20.00

HOW TO SELF-PUBLISH YOUR BOOK AND HAVE THE FUN
AND EXCITEMENT OF BEING A BEST-SELLING AUTHOR
by Melvin Powers

An expert's step-by-step guide to marketing your book successfully   176 Pages ... $20.00

A NEW GUIDE TO RATIONAL LIVING
by Albert Ellis, Ph.D. & Robert A. Harper, Ph.D.

. How Far Can You Go With Self-Analysis? 2. You Feel the Way You Think 3. Feeling Well by
Thinking Straight 4. How You Create Your Feelings 5. Thinking Yourself Out of Emotional
Disturbances 6. Recognizing and Attacking Neurotic Behavior 7. Overcoming the Influences
of the Past 8. Does Reason Always Prove Reasonable? 9. Refusing to Feel Desperately
Unhappy 10. Tackling Dire Needs for Approval 11. Eradicating Dire Fears of Failure
2. How to Stop Blaming and Start Living 13. How to Feel Undepressed though Frustrated
4. Controlling Your Own Destiny 15. Conquering Anxiety   256 Pages ... $7.00

PSYCHO-CYBERNETICS
A New Technique for Using Your Subconscious Power
by Maxwell Maltz, M.D., F.I.C.S.

. The Self Image: Your Key to a Better Life 2. Discovering the Success Mechanism Within
You 3. Imagination—The First Key to Your Success Mechanism 4. Dehypnotize Yourself
from False Beliefs 5. How to Utilize the Power of Rational Thinking 6. Relax and Let Your
Success Mechanism Work for You 7. You Can Acquire the Habit of Happiness 8. Ingredients
of the Success-Type Personality and How to Acquire Them 9. The Failure Mechanism: How
to Make It Work For You Instead of Against You 10. How to Remove Emotional Scars, or
How to Give Yourself an Emotional Face Lift 11. How to Unlock Your Real Personality
2. Do-It-Yourself Tranquilizers   288 Pages ... $7.00

A PRACTICAL GUIDE TO SELF-HYPNOSIS
by Melvin Powers

. What You Should Know About Self-Hypnosis 2. What About the Dangers of Hypnosis?
3. Is Hypnosis the Answer? 4. How Does Self-Hypnosis Work? 5. How to Arouse Yourself
from the Self-Hypnotic State 6. How to Attain Self-Hypnosis 7. Deepening the Self-Hypnotic
State 8. What You Should Know About Becoming an Excellent Subject 9. Techniques for
Reaching the Somnambulistic State 10. A New Approach to Self-Hypnosis When All Else
Fails 11. Psychological Aids and Their Function 12. The Nature of Hypnosis 13. Practical
Applications of Self-Hypnosis   128 Pages ... $3.00

The books listed above can be obtained from your book dealer or directly from Melvin Powers.
When ordering, please remit $2.00 postage for the first book and 50¢ for each additional book.

Melvin Powers
12015 Sherman Road, No. Hollywood, California 91605

NOTES